SUBOTAI THE VALIANT
GENGHIS KHAN'S
GREATEST GENERAL

Richard A. Gabriel

PRAEGER

Westport, Connecticut
London

Library of Congress Cataloging-in-Publication Data

Gabriel, Richard A.

    Subotai the Valiant: Genghis Kahn's greatest general / Richard A. Gabriel.
       p. cm.
    Includes bibliographical references and index.
    ISBN 0–275–97582–7 (alk. paper)
    1. Sabutai, ca. 1172–1245. 2. Genghis Khan, 1162–1227.
3. Mongols—History. I. Title.
  DS19.G34   2004
  950'.21'092—dc22   2004049563

British Library Cataloguing in Publication Data is available.

Library of Congress Catalog Card Number: 2004049563
ISBN: 0–275–97582–7

First published in 2004

Praeger Publishers, 88 Post Road West, Westport, CT 06881
An imprint of Greenwood Publishing Group, Inc.
www.praeger.com

Printed in the United States of America

The paper used in this book complies with the
Permanent Paper Standard issued by the National
Information Standards Organization (Z39.48–1984).

10 9 8 7 6 5 4 3 2 1

In Memoriam

Steven Charles Krantz

*father, husband, brother, teacher, musician
and son—a very good man indeed*

CONTENTS

ILLUSTRATIONS

PREFACE

S ubotai *bagatur*, that is to say, Subotai the Valiant, was one of the greatest generals in ancient military history. He was surely the equal of Hannibal and Scipio in tactical brilliance, and stands with Alexander and Caesar as a strategist. He commanded armies whose size, scale, and scope of operations surpassed most of those of the ancient world. Under his leadership and direction, Mongol armies moved faster and over longer distances with a greater scope of maneuver than any armies had done before. The Muslim chroniclers tell us that when he died at age seventy-three, Subotai "had conquered thirty-two nations and won sixty-five pitched battles." His fame was such that after his death both his Chinese and Muslim enemies erected monuments to him. Indeed, had there been no Subotai the Valiant, there would have been no Mongol conquest of Korea, China, Persia, and Russia—nor of Hungary, the conquest of which by Subotai's armies destroyed every remaining military force standing between the Mongol advance and Europe. Had not the Great Khan died (an event that required the Mongol armies and their princes to return to Mongolia to elect a successor), there is every likelihood that Subotai would have destroyed Europe itself!

It is surprising, therefore, that Subotai remains almost unknown in the West for the great strategist and tactical genius that he was. Although Giovanni di Plano Carpini wrote an account of the Mongol army, its equipment, and its tactics in 1248 as a result of his visit to the Mongol court, this work appears to have had no influence whatsoever on European military thought or practice. Nor did the writings of Marco Polo. Jean Pierre Abel Remusat, writing in 1829, offered a nine-page "biography" of Subotai in the form of a translation of a Chinese record. Hans Delbruck's magnificent work, *The History of the Art of War*, fails to mention the Mongols at all. As far as I can tell, the first modern military historian to write an analysis of Mongol military practice that included some treatment of Subotai's campaigns was the Russian Lieutenant General Mikhail I. Ivanin (1801–1874). Given the Russian experience with the Mongol and Turkic tribes in Central Asia at the time, the work was immediately recognized as an important contribution to military thought. The book and the study of Mongol military methods were incorporated into the curriculum of the Imperial Military Academy and other (Soviet) military schools until after World War II. In the West proper, however, military historians and practitioners virtually ignored Mongol military history and remained ignorant of the achievements of its greatest general, Subotai. In 1927, Sir Basil H. Liddell-Hart devoted a chapter of his *Great Captains Unveiled* to Genghis Khan in which he offers a sketch of Subotai's achievements. Henry Morel, a French military historian, authored an article on the Mongols in 1922, and in 1932, a Canadian officer contributed a small monograph on the subject in which Subotai is mentioned in passing. Thus, one of the greatest generals in all history has remained almost completely unknown in the West.

Subotai the Valiant is, therefore, the first attempt at a military biography of the great general to be published in the West. In the attempt, I have relied primarily upon English translations of Arabic, Persian, Chinese, and French sources for my information. Using English translations of *The Secret History of the Mongols* as well, I have sought in one way or another to incorporate every piece of information that can reasonably be garnered from the original sources. I have also used such bits and pieces about Subotai as are to be found scattered in secondary sources to assemble as complete a portrait of this great general as the information itself will permit. Even if my effort has fallen short, there is now, at the minimum, a single source to which students of Mongol and military history may turn to learn more about one of history's superb field commanders. For Subotai is more than a historical figure; his legacy is, in fact, living history. For much of the theory and practice of modern military operations was first used by Subotai and his Mongol armies. The modern emphasis on speed, maneuver, surprise, envelopment, the rear battle, deep battle, and the battle of annihilation all first emerged as an identifiable tactical skill set in the campaigns of Subotai. In this sense, it can be said that those who would master today's battles would do well first to study the battles of the past.

1 SUBOTAI THE VALIANT

The old blacksmith and his two sons struggled through the knee-deep snow, making their way down the steep mountainside toward Temujin's camp. The three of them had come a long way from the dark forest of the *taiga* west of Lake Baikal that was their home. Up ahead, within sight, was the tree line, where the snow gave way to bare ground and rock. Another few *li* and they would reach the steppe itself, where the spring temperatures had already begun to turn the Mongolian plain green with new grass. It was spring, the time of year when the Mongol clans left their winter camps in the mountains and drove their horse herds down to the steppes, where the half-starved animals that had survived the brutal Mongolian winter could eat their fill and replenish their bodies. It would take at least a month before the horses were healthy enough to permit their use in that favorite Mongol pastime: war.

The old man's name was Jarchigudai. He was an Uriangkhai, one of the forest tribes that lived in the mountains and thick forests north of the Mongolian steppe. Twenty years ago, he had made this same journey. Then he had come with his first-born son, Jelme, now a strapping young man of eighteen summers. Jarchigudai had been a blacksmith then, as he still was, and he carried his blacksmith's bellows on his back when he came to see Yesugei, the warrior and heir to the Mongol dynasty that had once ruled all the Mongol clans. He had come then to offer Yesugei his first-born as his servant. Yesugei had been camped at Deligun Hill on the Onan River, where his wife had presented him with a son of his own.[1] Yesugei had named his first-born, Temujin, after a brave warrior that Yesugei had slain in one of the interminable battles between the clans. Jarchigudai's son had then also been an infant, having been born in the same month as Temujin. Yesugei had welcomed Jarchigudai's gift with gratitude, but feared that his wife could not care properly for two infants. So he had sent the blacksmith away with the promise that when Jelme had grown to be a man, Yesugei would welcome him into his service. So Jarchigudai the blacksmith returned to his people in the forest where, over the years, he had plied his trade as Jelme had grown to manhood. During this time, Jarchigudai's wife had given him another son, but the effort had killed her, and Jarchigudai was alone in the world, except for his two boys.

Then word was brought to Jarchigudai that Yesugei had been killed by the Tartars, poisoned as they falsely offered him the hospitality of the Mongol tent. With Yesugei dead, the young Temujin, barely ten years old, had not been able to hold the loyalty of the warriors in the clan. He, his brothers, and his mother had been abandoned on the steppe without horses when the clan gave their loyalty to new leaders. For some years Temujin and his family had survived and rebuilt their fortunes until, only a year before Jarchigudai had learned of Yesugei's death, Temujin had formed an alliance with his father's *anda*, or blood brother, who in turn brought Temujin under his protection. With this friendship, Temujin, a prince of royal Mongol blood, had begun to attract other men and their families to him. Now, in the spring of 1187, as he camped on the banks of the Onan, Temujin was the leader of a small group of followers, families, and herds. Jarchigudai knew that Temujin was the son of a royal father and heir to the old Mongol dynasty. To a simple man like the blacksmith, a promise was a promise. As he had promised to bring his son to Yesugei when the time was right, so now he travelled a great distance to keep his promise to the son of the man to whom he had given his word.

Jarchigudai and his sons reached the camp late in the morning, when the heat of the steppe had already driven the cool morning air away. Temujin was waiting in front of his tent, having been warned of the strangers' approach by his sentries. He must have wondered who these travelers were and was on his guard, for the life of a Mongol warrior in those days was perilous indeed. As the *Secret History of the Mongols* tells the story, Jarchigudai spoke to Temujin:

> "Many years ago, I had a son, Jelme, who was born when you were born and grew up when you grew up. When your people were camped at Deligun Hill on the Onan, when you, Temujin, were born, I gave your father a sable blanket to swaddle you in."[2] The old man could see from the expression on Temujin's face that it was the first time he had heard such a tale

about his own youth. Every Mongol knew his lineage back at least five generations and could recite it at a moment's notice. But this, Jarchigudai sensed, Temujin had not known. The old blacksmith went on. "When you were an infant, I also gave my son, Jelme, to your father, but since he was just an infant then I kept him with me."[3] He paused and looked at Jelme, who, he knew, was eager to join Temujin's clan. Since boyhood, Jelme had shown neither aptitude nor interest in becoming a blacksmith. Jarchigudai turned back to Temujin. "Now," he said, "I have come to keep my promise to your father. Now Jelme is yours, to put on your saddle and open your door." Then he gave Temujin his son.[4]

The *Secret History* tells us nothing about Jelme's younger brother, then ten years old and standing behind his father watching everything that transpired. As the youngest son, he would become the *ochigin*, or "keeper of the hearth," for it was the custom of the forest tribes to place the father's estate in the trust of the youngest son. With Jelme gone, old Jarchigudai expected his youngest to become a blacksmith, for that was the way of the Uriangkhai. We do not know what the young boy thought as he watched. Perhaps he was struck by the physical presence of Temujin, a man taller than most Mongols, of powerful build, and with stone-gray eyes—like a wolf's, it was said. He had never been out of the forests, and perhaps he was impressed with the openness and beauty of the springtime steppe, with its green carpet of new grass, or with the heat of the sun that he could feel shining directly upon his body, unimpeded by the trees of the thick forests in his own land. Or perhaps he was like his brother in ways his father did not know, in that he had never wished to be a blacksmith. Now that Jelme had found another life for himself, perhaps he, too, might one day seek another way. But all this is uncertain. What is certain is that the meeting between Temujin and the sons of Jarchigudai the blacksmith in the early spring of 1187 was to have enormous consequences for the world. In less than twenty years, the young warrior-prince Temujin would come to unite and rule a new nation composed of "all the people whose tents are protected by skirts of felt."[5] Chosen in the year 1206 by a vast conclave of all the tribes of Mongolia, Temujin was given a new name, one that would make the world tremble. On that May field long ago, Temujin, once the outlaw, became Genghis Khan. The younger of Jarchigudai's boys, too, would one day make the world shake. Jarchigudai's youngest son did indeed disappoint his father. When he was fourteen years old, the time when a Mongol boy became a warrior, he left the land of the Uriangkhai to join the army of

Temujin. The boy's name was Subotai, and he became one of the greatest generals in history.

One of the more interesting paradoxes of military history is that the greatest Mongol general of them all was not, strictly speaking, a Mongol at all. The term *Mongol* refers to the group of clans that constituted the tribe from which Genghis Khan came. Once he had unified the other tribes of Mongolia—the Kerits, Merkits, Naimans, Tartars, etc.—the general confederation was given the common name of Mongols by Chinese, Muslim, and Christian chroniclers. All the tribes were nomadic steppe people who moved their horse and cattle herds with the seasons in search of pasture. All were horsemen and all shared the same type and method of warfare in that they were horse-borne bowmen. The Uriangkhai, to which Subotai belonged, was among the clans called forest tribes or, somewhat less correctly, forest Mongols. The chroniclers knew the Uriangkhai as the Reindeer People, and they lived in the forest taiga of the upper Yenisei River near the western edge of Lake Baikal.[6] They lived a vastly different life from that of the Mongol warriors of the steppe, considering themselves separate from them. Indeed, when Genghis Khan came to power, he quickly sent several military expeditions against the forest tribes to bring them under his control.

Genghis' interest in the forest tribes stemmed less from any feeling of consanguinity than from stark steppe economics. The Uriangkhai were hunters and fishermen who lived by trapping and trading Siberian furs to the steppe Mongols, who valued them highly as clothing against the harsh Mongolian winters. When hunting, the Uriangkhai wore "small, well-polished bones tied to their feet, with which they speed so swiftly over the ice that they catch animals in flight."[7] The Uriangkhai were not pastoral; that is, they did not move seasonally with the herds, but lived in clustered villages in permanent log huts covered with hides and birch bark. This stability led some of them to become metal smiths, some of whom traveled to the Mongol seasonal encampments where they practiced their trade repairing metal weapons and household implements. Jarchigudai was one of these smiths.

The climate of the Siberian taiga is much colder and snowier, and it has less daylight than the Mongolian steppe, so the Uriangkhai used animal skins for clothing more than did the steppe peoples. If we can trust the description of the Persian physician Rashid ad-Din, writing in his *Jami'at-Tavarikh* (*Great Collection of Histories*) around 1300, the forest tribes took no part in the tribal wars of the steppe Mongols. Rashid wrote that these tribes usually kept no herds, except for the Uriangkhai, who maintained domesticated herds of reindeer that they called *reem*.[8] Their descendants, the Reindeer People, still survive in the forests of Siberia, near the Arctic Circle, living much as they did during Subotai's time. According to Rashid, the forest tribes rarely left their woodlands:

> They believe that there is no happier life than their own. Their country being very cold, they hunt much over the snow. They bind to their feet long lengths of wood that they call *chana*, using their staffs in their hands to push them along in the snow, like the pole of a boat. They shoot down mountainsides so swiftly that they catch up with animals. . . . This is something you must see, in order to believe it.[9]

As the son of a blacksmith in the Siberian taiga, Subotai was raised much differently than the son of a steppe Mongol. Unlike the boys of the steppe, Subotai was not taught to ride by his mother at age three; he was not given a bow and instruction in its use by age five. Whereas the steppe Mongol spent most of his life on horseback, it is likely that Subotai had never even ridden a horse until he joined Genghis' army at age fourteen. Nor had Subotai any experience in spending long hours in the saddle in the alternating cold and heat of the Mongolian steppe while the entire tribe moved across the open plain with few landmarks to guide it. He possessed no sense of the wide expanse of the steppe or even a sense of distance. It is doubtful that anything from his life in the thick, mountainous forests would have prepared him for the sheer nakedness of the steppe or the desert, or for the terrible sense of vulnerability that can come with it. Unlike the sons of the steppe, this son of the taiga had no experience in eating uncooked food, drinking *kumis*, or drinking the blood of his horse for nourishment to sustain him on a long march. It is unlikely that, accustomed to life in the forests, he possessed that unique Mongol ability to spot movement in the open plain miles before it was upon you, or the ability to tell the difference between a man and animal at such great distances. For anyone lacking these abilities, the steppe became a dangerous place where a surprise attack could descend quickly upon the unwary, often with deadly results. Yet this son of a blacksmith somehow became the greatest general in Mongol history. His exploits rank him with the most successful of generals in all of human history. Just how this came to be is a very interesting tale.

Writing in his *Historia Mongalorum quos nos Tartaros appellamus* in 1248, the Franciscan monk Giovanni di Plano Carpini, who had returned from his papal mission to the Mongol court in 1247, recorded that Subotai, thought of by the Mongols as their greatest general, was still alive and well.[10] The Chinese biography of Subotai included in the *Sou Houng Kian Lou* (translated by Jean Pierre Abel Remusat in 1829) says that the great general died at the age of seventy-three.[11] Accordingly, we may place the dates of Subotai's life from 1175 to 1248. The first mention of Subotai in any source occurs in *The Secret History of the Mongols*, the great saga of the Mongol people that records the rise and life of Genghis Khan. Written in poetic form, the *Secret History* is to Mongol history and myth as the *Iliad* is to the Greek.[12] We first hear of Subotai in connection with the tale of the break between Temujin and his powerful and jealous ally, Jamuga. For more than a year, the two had been allies, and even anda (blood brothers). Their clans traveled and camped together. Eventually, however, as Jamuga became suspicious of Temujin's growing popularity, the two clans separated and no longer camped together. This signalled to all the clans and warriors of the Mongol tribe that the time had come to choose sides, and most chose Temujin: "People arrived from the Jalayir, from the Onggur and the Manghud. Ogele Cherbi, Borgorchu's kin, joined from the Arulad, and Jelme's younger brother, Subotai Bagatur, left the Uriangkhai to join them."[13]

Subotai had followed his brother's example, leaving the forests and his father's forge for a life of adventure in the service of Temujin the outlaw. Young men pretending to be old enough to join the military is a story as old as armies themselves are. By rough reckoning, Subotai was not yet fourteen, the age when a Mongol boy became a warrior.

The poem speaks of Subotai as bagatur, as if he had already possessed this title at the time he joined Temujin. The title itself means brave or valiant, thus Subotai the Valiant, as he was known to the Chinese chroniclers. The term found its way into Russian as *bogatyr*. It was the title of the Mongol knight and was acquired by Subotai as a young officer serving in Temujin's bodyguard. *The Secret History* was written sometime between 1240 and 1260, when Subotai was already well known as a talented general and had already been granted this title. Although Subotai rose to higher rank, throughout his life he used the title of bagatur most often—so much so that foreign chroniclers often mistakenly thought it to be the great general's surname!

When Subotai joined Temujin, he was but a young boy and surely no knight. He was Jelme's younger brother, however, and Jelme had become one of Temujin's closest comrades and advisors. Jelme had come to Temujin when he was at a difficult juncture. Outlawed by the chief of his own clan, his horses stolen, and his wife kidnapped by the Merkits, Temujin had few warriors to stand by him. The esteem in which Jelme was held by Temujin is clear in the *Secret History*. In 1188, when the clans chose Temujin to be their leader in war, all the clan leaders came forward to pledge their loyalty to Temujin. The only exceptions were Jelme and Bogorchu. To stress the esteem in which these two companions were held, the poem tells of Temujin pledging his loyalty and honor to them.

> Then Temujin turned to Borgorchu [*sic*] and Jelme and said, "You two, from the time when there was no one to fight beside me but my own shadow, you were my shadow and gave my mind rest. That will always be in my thoughts. From the time when there was nothing to whip my horses with except their tails, you were their tails and gave my heart peace. That will always be in my heart. Since you were the first two who came to my side, you will be chieftains over all the rest of the people."[14]

We may reasonably assume from this that Jelme was privy to all the consultation and planning sessions that Temujin held with his officers as they sought to defeat their enemies both politically and on the battlefield. The use of the commander's conference, in which the leader gathers his trusted commanders and advisors to plan a campaign, has a very long history in the ancient West, and was commonly used by the Mongols as well.[15] It is likely that Jelme's position as a trusted comrade is what made Subotai's higher education in military matters possible.

That a young boy from the forests could adjust to Mongol life on the steppe is clear enough from Jelme's circumstances. Jelme himself was given to Temujin as a slave, "to put on your saddle and open your [tent] door," a clear indication that Jelme possessed no military skills at all at that time. A few years later, we find him fully acclimated to the life of the Mongol soldier. But Subotai was still only a boy, and not yet ready to become a soldier. What, then, were they to do with him? He could hardly be turned to common labor, or even to rough training at the hands of the troops. If what the poem tells us about Jelme applied as well to Subotai, then it is possible that Subotai was assigned to be Temujin's keeper of the tent door while he gradually learned the military skills of the Mongol soldier, perhaps under the careful tutelage of a Mongol officer. Subotai's special status is implied by the poem. Although of no military status whatsoever, Subotai was permitted to pledge his loyalty to Temujin along with the other clan leaders as if, somehow, he was already one of them. In Subotai's pledge, there is the sense of a boy strongly impressed by the possibility of adventure and even by the sight of Temujin—so much so that one may have reason to believe that Subotai was excessive in his willingness to become Temujin's subordinate. Whereas other clan chieftains compare their loyalty to their leader in heroic terms, likening themselves to bears and wolves, Subotai's pledge reveals no such sense of nobility or military prowess:

> Then Subotai promised him: "I'll be like a rat and gather up others I'll be like a black crow and gather great flocks. Like the felt blanket that covers the horse, I'll gather up soldiers to cover you. Like the felt blanket that guards the tent from the wind, I'll assemble great armies to shelter your tent."[16]

To compare oneself to a crow and a rat suggests a young man a bit too eager to serve his master in any way he is ordered. Subotai has no military skills to offer his chief, and so offers his determination to serve in any capacity, even those usually considered below the Mongol warrior. (One wonders what the other chiefs thought of a boy who would compare his worth to that of a rat, which was regarded by Mongol soldiers as having value only as food.) Subotai's being like a felt blanket that guards the tent from the wind is instructive, however, for that is exactly the task of the doorkeeper of the tent.

As Jelme's brother and keeper of Temujin's tent door, Subotai would have been present at the war councils and discussions of Temujin's officers; among them, of course, was Jelme. At the same time, we can reasonably surmise that Subotai spent some of his days taking instruction in the military arts of the Mongol soldier: how to ride a horse, shoot a bow, and practice in the maneuver and fire tactics of the Mongol cavalry. Over the next decade, Temujin and his clan engaged in a series of battles with the other tribes, as well as his chief rival and former ally, Jamuga. For the most part, these engagements produced no strategic decisions about unifying the Mongol nation or deciding who would lead it. During this time, Subotai probably received his first taste of battle, perhaps only as a common soldier, and then later as commander of an *arban* (a squad of 10 men) or *djaghoun* (company of 100 men). The *Secret History* is silent with regard to Subotai's military experience during this decade of war, but it is likely that the tribal conflicts served to educate Subotai in the Mongol way of war and to season him to the physical and psychological rigors of campaigning. It is only in 1197, at the end of this period, that the records reveal anything further about Subotai's performance in battle or his fitness for command.

History would suggest that more important than his experience on the battlefield was Subotai's exposure to the discussions held and questions asked in the commander's conferences by Temujin's highest-ranking commanders, Jelme among them. There is no reason to suspect that Subotai was not present at these conferences, perhaps at first only as an accidental observer and then, at some point when his military skills had improved, perhaps sitting behind Jelme while the discussions went on. Ten years of listening to the plans and arguments of senior commanders as they planned their campaigns and subsequently dissected the performance of the men in after-action reports would have given the young Subotai an excellent and very practical military education. Here he would have learned to think beyond unit tactics; to see how the tactical employment of units fit into the larger plan of the campaign, and how they in turn fit into the overall strategy. Although his own field experience at this time would have permitted him to command only smaller units, Subotai was exposed to the planning and execution of war at the operational level. The ability to conceptualize war plans and implement them on a grand scale is one of the most difficult skills for any officer to acquire. Most never acquire this ability, something that may explain why warfare has, over the long centuries of its practice, produced only a few truly great generals. Subotai became one of those generals. His military education was unique. While he was gaining experience in different levels of tactical command, he was simultaneously being exposed over a long period to the discussions, planning, and analysis of battles at the highest levels of command.

As events unfolded, it was Subotai's education rather than his battlefield experience that shaped his intellect, with the result that he became one of the most successful and innovative generals in history. The closest that modern military establishments come to a military education of the type experienced by Subotai is, perhaps, the German General Staff system. There young officers, often captains, spend much of their careers in parallel staff and combat assignments at higher levels where they are continuously exposed to the deliberations of more senior commanders.

In 1197, when Subotai was twenty-three years old and by now a soldier with some battlefield experience, Temujin undertook an attack against the rival Merkit tribe. According to the account of the war preserved for us by Chinese chroniclers, Subotai was placed in command of a small unit, most likely a djaghoun of 100 soldiers. Up to this time there were no units in the Mongol army larger than the 1,000-man regiments (*mingan*), command of which was always placed in the hands of Temujin's senior commanders. The Chinese records offer the following account of Subotai's role in the war with the Merkits:

> Temujin convoked an assembly of his officers to march against the Merkits. He asked . . . "Who will be the first to attack?" Subotai volunteered and Temujin, noting his courage, offered to send a corps of 100 elite soldiers along with him. But Subotai opposed this saying, "I will take care of everything." Then Subotai traveled to the Merkit camp and feigned abandoning Temujin's cause. They [the Merkits] placed such confidence in what Subotai told them that they neglected to make sufficient preparation so that when the great Mongol army arrived at the Tchen River they were taken by surprise, and two of their generals were captured.[17]

Subotai's presence at a commander's conference of senior officers planning the Merkit attack suggests that, although he was a junior officer, he had become somewhat of a regular attendee at these meetings. The fact that Subotai was permitted to participate fully in the discussions implies that over the years, Subotai, although not an experienced or distinguished field commander as far as we can judge, was nonetheless regarded by Temujin himself as a valuable source of military counsel. Other men had their courage and physical stamina to offer their commander-in-chief. It was becoming evident that Subotai had something much rarer to offer: a brilliant military mind.

The tale of Subotai's actions against the Merkits offers the first glimpse into his thinking. What is impressive is his use of deception and surprise, two qualities that repeatedly characterized his future campaigns. Subotai's armies repeatedly led the enemy into thinking one thing while he was preparing to do the opposite. And when his armies struck, they almost always achieved strategic or tactical surprise. As at the Tchen River against the Merkits, whenever the major blow fell, it always fell at a single point—the *Schwerpunkt*—where the main army arrived at a single location to concentrate their force. Many times Subotai fought against armies larger than his own, but he always maneuvered to insure that when the final blow was struck, he unfailingly achieved numerical superiority at the decisive point. The Chinese account of Subotai's actions against the Merkits reveals his willingness to attempt military operations marked by boldness and risk. Although he became known for his detailed planning and attention to intelligence reports, at base Subotai possessed the soul of a gambler, which, as Napoleon remarked, was the most important trait of a great general. Once he had mastered what he could, Subotai was always willing, as the poet said, to risk his winnings on "one turn of pitch-and-toss."[18] These traits of character, when joined with a first-rate intellect, made Subotai an extraordinarily innovative and imaginative commander.[19]

Between 1197 and 1206 (when he at last defeated his rivals), Temujin fought a series of battles in which Subotai took part. In 1201, Temujin fought a number of indecisive skirmishes against Jamuga and the Oga Khan. In one of these, Temujin was wounded in the neck by an arrow. The faithful Jelme sucked the wound until it clotted and saved the life of his friend and leader. In 1202, Temujin conducted a campaign against the Tartars. Unlike the previous campaign in 1199, this time Temujin put an end to the Tartar threat by having each Tartar male "measured against the linchpin." All the captured Tartar males were led past the wheel of a wagon. Those who were taller than the linchpin of the wheel were beheaded; the smaller children were spared, and later taken into the Mongol armies.[20] The women and young girls were turned to slavery. This practice was fairly common among the Mongols, but no one had ever employed it on such a scale before. The result was that the Tartars ceased to exist as a separate tribe.

In 1203, Jamuga and the Oga Kahn had raised a large army from the remaining tribes and brought Temujin to battle at a place called the Red Willows. Badly outnumbered, Temujin's army fought the enemy coalition to a draw but suffered such heavy casualties that Temujin was forced to withdraw. Of the almost 20,000 men in Temujin's army who fought in the Battle of the Red Willows, only 2,600 were alive at the end of the day. Temujin and what was left of his army retreated to the northeast, finally stopping at a small lake known as Baljuna. The epic poem tells us that,

> As to those of the Mongols who have stayed with Temujin, their plight is such that they have now but one horse to each rider [usually three], no lead horses or pack animals, [the baggage train was captured] and that instead of tents all they have for shelter is the trees of the forest.[21]

The conditions at Baljuna were no better. At this time of year, the lake was almost dry, and what water there was had to be squeezed from a handful of mud.[22] Only a few of Temujin's officers remained with him, among them the loyal Subotai. It was the Mongol custom to abandon a leader in defeat and seek new accommodations. Temujin never forgot the loyal few who stood beside him in his darkest hour. Like the men around Mao Tse Tung on his long march to Yunan or the "precious few" who stood with Henry at

Agincourt, for the rest of his life those who had been at Baljuna were always closest to the Great Khan. He created a special military order for them, the Order of the Ter-Khans, and they were rewarded with wealth and position. Each was permitted to commit nine capital offenses without punishment and was free to enter Genghis' tent at any time. Temujin's gratitude for his comrades was expressed in a Persian account:

> Moved by the loyalty of those who had not left him in his distress, he promised them, hands clasped and eyes raised to heaven, that hence-forth he would share with them the sweet and the bitter, asking that, if he went back on his word, he might become as the muddy water of the Baljuna. As he spoke, he drank of this water and passed the cup to his officers, who swore in their turn never to leave him. These companions of Genghis Khan were known afterwards as the Baljunians, and were recompensed magnificently for their loyal adherence.[23]

Among these precious few was Subotai, who, true to his original oath taken long ago, stood by his commander and protected him from the wind that was blowing violently across Mongolia.

Less than a year later, after he had rallied his clans and rebuilt his army, Temujin attacked the Oga Khan, taking his army by surprise and trapping it in a narrow pass. This time there would be no mistake. Although the Oga Khan and his son escaped, the army of the Kerits was destroyed. Temujin then captured the remainder of the Kerits and dispersed them into his ranks as slaves so that the Kerits ceased to exist as a separate people. Thus, in the winter of 1203–1204, Temujin had become master of all eastern and central Mongolia. Only the Naimans in the west remained. In the summer of 1204, the Year of the Rat, Temujin

> divided his army to form troops of thousands, and having appointed his commanders, having chosen his eighty night guards and seventy soldiers as day guards. . . . And having sprinkled libations of mare's milk on his stan-dard of nine tails as a signal to Heaven that he was going to war, he set out with his army against the Naiman.[24]

The army numbered 80,000 men.

Temujin proceeded cautiously on his approach to the Naiman territory. He knew the Naimans would outnumber him when the time came to give battle. Their warriors had a fierce reputation, their commanders known for their tendency to take the offensive and press the attack. But Temujin also knew that the Naiman king, Baibuka Tayang, was not a good general. Long before the present war he had taken the measure of the man and concluded that, "the Naiman are strong in numbers, but their khan is a weak man who has never been out of his tent."[25] When in command of a strong army, even a weak general can be dangerous, however, for as an old proverb had it, an army of lions led by a donkey was more dangerous than an army of donkeys led by a lion! And so when Temujin approached the land of the Naiman, he ordered that when his army camped at night each man was to light five campfires so that anyone watching would think the army was greater in numbers than it was.

The Naiman generals wanted to attack Temujin immediately. It was the end of May, the time when the Mongols leave their mountain encampments and come down to the plains, where the horses can feed on the thick new grass and rebuild their bodies, which have grown thin, weak, and hollow-flanked from almost six months of fast. For at least a month, the horses are of no use in war, and it was at this time that Temujin's army was most vulnerable. But when the Naiman Tayang received reports of the number of fires flickering in Temujin's camp, he became fearful that he was facing a larger army than his own and took counsel of his fears. The Tayang resisted the entreaties of his commanders to attack. He proposed instead to undertake a strategic retreat, forcing the Mongols to follow on their already exhausted mounts.

> If we take our people back over the Altai [mountains] retreating in order this way, reforming our army on the other side of the passes, marching back and forth and enticing them to follow, appearing to retreat from them but still fighting small skirmishes along the way . . . the Mongol horses will be exhausted by then and we'll throw our army back in their faces.[26]

It was a sound (if cautious) plan, one befitting a general who "had never been out of his tent." The debate among the Tayang's generals went on for more than a month until the *senggum*, the son of the Tayang, put an end to it with his eagerness to attack and convinced his father. So "the Naiman swept down the Tamir River Valley, crossing the Orkhon, passing the eastern edge of Mount Nakhu. As they came to the Chakirmagud, they were seen by Temujin's sentries."[27] The delay had served Temujin well. His horses were fit and his army was ready for war, and his sentries had deprived the Naiman of the element of surprise.

The Mongol epic describes the battle in detail and provides us for the first time with an account of Subotai's performance in battle as commander of a 1,000-man mingan (or regiment) fighting as part of a four-regiment task force commanded by Jebe. The tactical orders of the Mongols have come down to us, so that the order of march was to be "as thick as grass," perhaps a reference to marching in solid regimental column to withstand an attack or to maximize shock in the attack.[28] Once on the battlefield, the units were to assume "the lake formation" and were to attack "drill-wise."[29] Unfortunately, we do not know to what formations and tactics these terms refer. Aware that the Naiman had a reputation for offensive action, Temujin order his advanced guard immediately into the attack. The impression of the text is that he caught the enemy off-guard as it was assembling its units prior to battle on the open plain. The spoiling attack was successful, and

> our forward troops drove the Naiman back from Chakirmagud. Their forces retreated from us, reforming before Mount Nakhu on the skirts of the mountains there. Our forward troops drove them back, herding them together into a great mass before Mount Nakhu.[30]

As in the *Iliad*, the Mongol epic describes the great battle through the eyes of the commander who, located on the high ground behind his army, watches the armies assemble and the battle unfold before him. The Naiman Tayang inquires of his ally, Jamuga,

> Who are these people who charge us like wolves pursuing so many sheep, chasing the sheep right into the flock? Jamuga replies, "These are the Four Dogs of my *anda* Temujin. They feed on human flesh and are tethered with an iron chain. They have foreheads of brass, their jaws are like scissors, their tongues like piercing awls, their heads are iron, their whipping tails, swords. They feed on dew. Running, they ride on the back of the wind. In the day of battle, they devour enemy flesh. Behold, they are now unleashed, and they slobber at the mouth with glee. These four dogs are Jebe, and Kublai, Jelme, and Subotai."[31]

Frightened at the ferocity of the attack, the Naiman ordered his army to withdraw up the mountain.

Here we find the first mention of Subotai as a battlefield commander, his regiment operating in concert with three others. The accounts of Genghis' later wars mention the use of such special units as the Four Dogs from time to time. We hear of these units in other battles when their commanders are called the Four Torrents, the Four Courses, and the Four Heroes. That Temujin chose his commanders purely on ability and experience is evident in the fact that none of the Four Dogs at the battle of Chakirmagud were of his own tribe. Khubilai was a prince of another tribe, Jebe was of the Tayichigud clan, and Jelme and Subotai were Uriangkhai. Subotai's command of a regiment at Chakirmagud is evidence that he had shown himself to be a competent combat commander as well as a military thinker. It is also obvious from the poem that the Four Dogs were superb battlefield commanders whose units were known for their ferocity in the attack. At the battle of Chakirmagud they seem to have been used as mobile shock troops, much like a modern armored column, to drive through the enemy ranks at different points, penetrate to the rear, and disrupt the enemy formations. The text tells us in this regard that they "charge us like wolves pursuing so many sheep, chasing the sheep right into the flock." It is also likely that one of their missions was to attack the enemy commander and disrupt his ability to command. Students of modern war will recognize these tactics as part of the "deep battle," a concept invented by the Mongols and, as we shall see, transmitted to the future armies of the West.

The battle raged all that day with the Naiman getting the worst of it until they were forced to retreat up Mount Nakhu and darkness ended the fight. During the night, the Naiman attempted to escape:

> In the darkness the Naiman tried to drive their carts and horses back down and fell from the cliffs and narrow trails of Nakhu, their bodies falling atop one another, their bones shattering from the fall, their bodies crushing each other like piles of dead trees, and that's how most of them died.[32]

Come daylight, Temujin resumed the attack, surrounding the Tayang and his commanders, who died fighting to the last man even as the dishonorable Jamuga made his escape. As for the Naiman tribe, the text tells us that "they were assembled at the foot of the Altai and were disposed of,"[33] perhaps "measured by the linchpin" as the Tartars had been. The last major obstacle to Temujin's ambitions in Mongolia was destroyed at Chakirmagud. Only a few pockets of resistance remained. Later that year, Temujin attacked the Merkits and defeated them. The sons of the Merkit king escaped, however, and in the following year, the Year of the Ox (1205), Temujin ordered Subotai to hunt down the last of the Merkit princes and their followers and destroy them.

The *Secret History*'s account of Subotai's campaign is rich in detail, some of it confusing and requiring explanation. The difficulty arises immediately at the beginning of the poem, which tells us: "During the Year of the Ox Temujin sent out Subotai equipping his army with iron carts, to pursue the sons of Toghtogat Beki [Toqto'a Beki] and their followers."[34] The phrase *temur-tergen* is translated by Kahn and Cleaves as "iron carts," while Grousset translates it as "iron-framed wagons,"[35] from which Grousset suggests that they were special wagons built to withstand the rough terrain and gorges over which Subotai would have had to travel in his pursuit of the Merkits. This argument is unconvincing in light of the fact that the Mongols routinely conducted campaigns over such rough terrain and there are no other indications of iron carts before the Merkit campaign or after it. The reference to iron carts is puzzling, but may tell us something about the use of iron in the early Mongol armies.

In the Mongolian wars, Temujin's armies probably made only limited use of iron weapons and implements. For the most part, arrows and lances were made from fire-hardened wood, and the "arrow knife" used for manufacturing these weapons and keeping their tips sharp is mentioned several times in the *Secret History*. Armor and helmets were made not of metal but of boiled leather, fashioned while wet and dried to shape. As a pastoral people, the Mongols were periodically on the move and lacked the stability of place that is usually associated with the practice of metallurgy. Instead, the Mongol tribes relied upon trade with the forest tribes to provide them with iron implements, while the traveling smiths, like Jarchigudai, came among them in the spring to repair their iron weapons and implements and sell them new ones. It is certain that some iron arrowheads and spear blades were in use during this period, for tales were told of Mongol women scouring the battlefield to retrieve these items. During the war with the Chin that began in 1206, the Mongols were exposed to the Chinese metal army. Thereafter, the Mongols began to adopt metal weapons, helmets, and iron in general on a large scale. In their wars with the Muslims and the West, the Mongols usually excluded metal smiths from their slaughter and shipped them back to Mongolia or distributed them among the army units where they could keep Mongol equipment in repair. The deportation of metal smiths was so extensive in Russia that it required more than two centuries for the craft to reestablish itself once the Mongols had departed.

Against this background, it is interesting to speculate what the *Secret History* may be telling us about the iron carts and their relationship to Subotai, the blacksmith's son. Perhaps Subotai introduced some new element to the Mongol armies. Two possibilities suggest themselves. The first is that the iron carts are mobile forges that the armies, fighting larger campaigns of longer duration over longer distances, now required to keep their increasingly large stock of iron weapons, armor, and other implements in good repair. Even though the use of iron weapons by Temujin's army was not extensive in 1205, the *Secret History* was written between 1240 and 1260, when iron weapons were in common use. The chronicler may have simply been writing about what he knew and attributed it to Subotai's time. This is a common occurrence among ancient chronicles. In the Bible, for example, "chariots of iron" are attributed to David's army when, in fact, they were not used then. The Biblical chronicler, writing perhaps four centuries after David—when the Assyrians had introduced large armored chariots with metal tire rims, thus "chariots of iron,"—simply modified the chronology and attributed them to David's army as well.[36]

A second possibility is that Subotai's knowledge of iron led him to suggest a way to solve a chronic problem of Mongol military mobility. Mongol wagons were equipped with solid, wooden wheels of the kind commonly found in ancient Sumer and Egypt from the time of the third millennium B.C.E. Spokeless and solid, they were easy to manufacture but subject to breakdown in difficult terrain, a problem that also plagued the armies of Sumer and Egypt. Mongol armies usually operated on the treeless steppe or in steep mountains, where the lack of trees made finding the wood to repair broken wagon wheels difficult. Subotai, as the son of a blacksmith, may have hit upon the solution of fabricating an iron rim for the wooden wheel, a solution long known in China and the West. An iron rim would strengthen the wheel and reduce breakage in rough terrain. The iron carts are mentioned only twice in the *Secret History*, and in both instances they are associated with Subotai.

R. P. Lister, in his history of Genghis Khan, offers yet another explanation regarding Subotai and the iron carts: "Subotai had swiftly grown to enormous stature and bulk; none of the steppe horses could carry him far, and he customarily travelled in an iron wagon."[37] Unfortunately, Lister does not cite any of the chroniclers in support of Subotai's obesity. Figure 1.1 is a portrayal of Subotai that appears in the Chinese *Sou-Houng-Kian-Lou* and is the only known rendering of the man to come down to us. Portrayed in the stance of an attacking tiger, no doubt to imply his ferocity in battle, the drawing does not suggest that Subotai was obese. Nor is the rendering out of

Figure 1.1   Chinese Portrayal of Subotai

proportion to the portrayals of other Mongol generals in the same chronicle. Moreover, the reference to Subotai and the iron carts appears in the *Secret History* as occurring in 1205, less than a year after Subotai and the Four Dogs performed so gallantly in the battle against the Naiman. Later, in 1221, we find Subotai and Jebe conducting a great cavalry raid around the Caspian Sea covering more than a thousand miles on horseback. Then again, in 1224, when Genghis summoned Subotai to his camp in central Asia, Subotai made a solitary journey of over 1,000 miles on horseback to comply with the Khan's order. None of these exploits would have been possible had Subotai been obese and required to travel in an iron-wagon.

Subotai was thirty years old when he was assigned his first high-level, independent combat command. Although he had proven himself a capable combat commander at the regimental level, he had never been in sole command of a large force of several regiments until he was assigned to hunt down the Merkit princes. All his previous experience had been in command of units that were part of larger operational forces under the overall command of others. With the order to capture the Merkits, Subotai was assigned his first large, independent command with instructions to undertake operations far from his home base. The Mongol epic goes into considerable detail regarding the instructions given to Subotai by Temujin himself. The first part of these instructions amounts to a heroic narration by Temujin urging Subotai to be determined and courageous. Temujin tells Subotai,

> If they [the Merkits] sprout wings and fly up toward heaven, you, Subotai, become a falcon and seize them in mid-air. If they become marmots and claw into the earth with their nails, you become an iron rod and bore through the earth to catch them. If they become fish and dive into the depths of the sea, you, Subotai, become a net, casting yourself over them and dragging them back.[38]

But it is the second part of Temujin's instructions to Subotai that is puzzling, for in it he seems to be instructing Subotai in the very basic application of Mongol military arts, something that we would have thought completely unnecessary for a commander of Subotai's rank and experience. Thus, Temujin instructs Subotai:

> I'm sending you off to cross high passes and ford great rivers. Keep in mind the distance you will have to travel and spare your horses so they don't get exhausted. Conserve their strength before its [sic] used up. When a gelding is already worn out, it's useless to spare him.[39]

Perhaps Temujin recalled that Subotai was not a steppe Mongol by birth, and that, until the Uriangkhai had joined him, horsemanship was unknown to Subotai. So basic a reminder to even a lower-ranking steppe Mongol officer would have seemed strange, indeed. On the other hand, the Mongol epic, like other epics, may include considerable detail only to enlighten or entertain the reader. Perhaps Temujin's "oration" to Subotai is of the type of similar orations found by battle commanders in other epics and is purely a poetic device.

Throughout the narrative Temujin continues to instruct Subotai in basic military arts. He tells Subotai how to sustain the army on the long march to the objective.

> Once you have used up your provisions, there is nothing to save. There will be a great deal of game to hunt on the way. Keep in mind how far you have to go and don't let the men ride off to hunt at their whim. Only hunt within limits . . . then set a limit on how much will be killed.[40]

Once more, he instructs Subotai on the proper use of horses: "See to it that your men keep their cruppers hanging loose on their mounts and the bit of the bridle out of their mouth, except when you hunt."[41] Loosened cruppers and bits not only reduce fatigue on the horses but also make it impossible for the horsemen to chase game on a whim. Next, Temujin tells Subotai that on a long march it is the commander's responsibility to insure that military discipline is maintained at all times. "Having established these rules see to it you seize and beat any man who breaks them. Any man that I know who ignores my decree, have him brought back to stand before me. Any man I don't know who ignores this decree, cut off his head where he stands."[42] Finally, Temujin cautions Subotai that the application of tactics must always be directed toward the higher strategic goal and that tactics must never be permitted to distract the commander from his strategic objective. "Though your army will divide beyond the great rivers, all must continue in pursuit of one goal. Though mountain ranges separate your men from each other, think of nothing else but this task."[43] Temujin's advice is sound, of course, but what is puzzling is why he felt it necessary to instruct a senior regimental commander—one whom he had come to rely upon for his strategic insight in the councils of war—in such basic matters. Elsewhere in the *Secret History*, we find Temujin giving tactical direction to his commanders, but nowhere do we find it in such detail and at so rudimentary a level as we do in the instructions to Subotai. Perhaps because Subotai was not a steppe Mongol, Temujin remained uncertain as to his fitness for higher independent command even though Temujin knew the value of Subotai's military mind. If so, then sending Subotai against the Merkits in command of his first large-scale, independent operation may well have been a test of his ability. The Mongol epic tells us that Subotai passed the test. "So Subotai the Brave, equipped with iron carts, was sent off to war . . . he overtook the sons of Toghtoga Beki [*sic*] by the banks of the Chui River, destroying their forces, and returned."[44]

While Subotai was destroying the remnants of the Merkits, Jebe was hunting down the last of the Naiman princes. Jamuga, too, was captured and put to death. In May of 1206, the Year of the Tiger, "having set in order the lives of all the people whose tents are protected by skirts of felt, the Mongol clans assembled at the head of the Onan. They raised a white standard of nine tails and proclaimed Temujin the Great Khan."[45] For the first time in almost fifty years, all the Mongol clans were united under the command of a single national leader, and his name was Genghis Khan. He immediately set about creating a national army. When the armies of the clans were combined, there was sufficient manpower to create ninety-five regiments of 1,000 men each, also known as the mingans. Genghis personally selected the regimental commanders and made them all *Mingan-u Noyan*, or Lords of the Regiments.[46] Among them was Subotai. In appointing his commanders, Genghis had special praise for the Four Dogs, Subotai among them. "'For me you have broken the necks of the strong and the backs of the athletic. When the order, "Forward!" sounded, you clove rocks and stemmed the wild torrent. On the day of battle, with such men before me,' cried Genghis Khan, 'I could rest assured.'"[47]

Regimental-strength units were traditional to the Mongol armies. But now, perhaps conscious of his plans for conquest, Genghis introduced new units of 10,000 men. These were the Mongol *toumans* that were to gain such fame in the forthcoming wars against the Chinese, Muslims, and ultimately the West. Genghis assigned command of one of the three new toumans to Bogorchu to command the Army of the Right, one to Mukhali to command the Army of the Left, and one to Nayaga to command the Army of the Center. But most importantly, Genghis said, "Let the two commanders, Jebe and Subotai, lead armies as large as they can gather."[48] Here the *Secret History* tells us that Jebe and Subotai were appointed as the first *orloks* of the new Mongol army. The term literally means "eagles," but in the context of the terminology of military command, Jebe and Subotai were appointed Field Marshals. From that day forward, no major military operation was planned or undertaken by Genghis Khan, or later by his son, Ogedai, in which the voice of Subotai was not heard.

Genghis' selection of these two officers to lead his army is evidence of what historians have recognized as his unfailing capacity to judge the character and ability of the men he selected for high office. Jebe and Subotai could not have been more opposite. Jebe was a dashing and reckless leader of men in battle with considerable combat experience even before he joined Temujin. During one of the battles with the Tayichigud clan, Temujin had his horse shot out from underneath him when an arrow struck it in the spine. Later, when the Tayichiguds had been driven from the field, a young warrior rode into Temujin's camp. It was Jebe, and he told Temujin that he had shot the horse. Jebe's bravery so impressed Temujin that he spared his life and made him one of his unit commanders. From that day forward, Jebe was among the bravest of Temujin's warriors whose exploits are celebrated in the *Secret History*.

The Mongol epic, by contrast, tells us little about the combat prowess of Subotai. Indeed, the text hints that Temujin had doubts about Subotai's ability to command men under fire even though he had performed well at the regimental level. But Temujin was a shrewd judge of men, and Subotai had been present at the war councils for many years, first as a boy observing as he tended the tent door and later, as the Chinese tell us, as a participant in the discussions. Temujin became increasingly impressed by Subotai's intellect and his grasp of strategy and tactics in operational planning. We cannot know, of course, how many wars, battles, and campaigns undertaken by Temujin in his quest to become Khan might have been influenced or even planned by Subotai, but it is likely that his influence was considerable. Temujin may once have harbored doubts about Subotai's fitness for field command. Courage and warrior spirit were qualities not in short supply among steppe warriors. Competent field commanders were easily available, but an officer who could plan and coordinate large-scale military operations across thousands of miles was a rarity. Temujin had no doubt watched Subotai's mind work over many years around the campfires where battles were planned. Now that Genghis Khan had established a Mongol national army, he appointed his most brilliant officer to lead it.

Many of Genghis Khan's campaigns from this time forward were planned at the strategic level by Subotai. Among the most important of these were the wars against the Chin (1211–1216), the westward campaign against the Muslim empire of Khwarizm (1219–1224), and the attack against Russia and the West (1237–1242), which are the subject of detailed analysis in the following chapters. In all of these campaigns, Subotai took the field to direct operations. To be sure, the last word as to design and implementation of the campaigns rested with Genghis himself. The planning, however, was done by Subotai and his staff. Later this staff comprised Chinese and Muslim experts, as well as Mongols. After Genghis' death, his son, Ogedai, seems to have left all of the military planning and oversight to Subotai. It was the practice of both Genghis and Ogedai to appoint royal princes as the nominal commanders of military operations while real authority rested with Subotai. In the campaign against Russia and the West, for example, Batu was the nominal commander of the army, but Subotai actually planned and directed the battles. In one instance when Subotai and Batu disagreed, Subotai carried the day. In another, Subotai refused to execute a direct order of his commander, implying that the young Batu had lost his courage. Genghis Khan and Ogedai knew the value of Subotai's brilliance and were not wont to squander it merely to soothe the ego of a royal prince.

2 THE MONGOL WAR MACHINE

The Mongol army, during the time of Genghis Khan and his successor sons, was the most efficient and effective military machine in the world. Under the guidance of a number of talented political and military leaders, the Mongol army destroyed every major military force between China and Central Europe that dared take the field against it. With few exceptions, each time the Mongol army engaged an enemy, it did so with a significant numerical disadvantage. In almost every major campaign, the Mongols had the further disadvantage of having to conduct operations at the end of very long lines of supply, often conceding to their adversaries significant advantages in logistics and means of defense. In some ways, even the military equipment of the Mongols was not up to the standards of its opponents, and few soldiers in the West would have easily submitted to the arduous way of life required of a soldier of the Great Khan. Despite all these factors, the armies of the Mongols were among the most successful in the history of warfare, surpassing in some respects the achievements of the armies of Alexander and Caesar.

Mongol society was organized along feudal lines. Each tribe was led by its own *khan*. Below the khan were the powerful barons called *noyans*, and below them were the *bagaturs*, the Mongol equivalent of knights. These constituted a military aristocracy similar to those found in Medieval Europe during the same period. Below the nobility were the majority of individual freemen. Below them were the slaves. At times entire clans that had suffered defeat in the interminable conflicts between tribes and clans were reduced to serfdom, in service to the victorious tribe. Each tribe was divided into patriarchal clans, each of which formed its own *ordu*. Ordu simply meant camp. In the West, the camp of the Mongols was associated with their invading armies, such that ordu became the word "horde." Thus, "the Mongol horde."

Traditionally, the clans within each Mongol tribe fought each other over slaves, women, horses, and grazing rights. Once Genghis had unified the clans, Mongol law forbade such conflicts and prescribed the penalty of death for violations. Thus Genghis brought peace to the entire Mongol nation, where constant internecine conflict had been the rule. The Mongol "nation" was really a coalition of various steppe tribes (the Merkits, Kereits, Tartars, and Naimans to mention only the largest), unified by Genghis Khan through force. Since the Great Khan's own tribe was called the Mongols, it became commonplace to refer to the various other tribes as Mongols as well. There were scores of clans and tribes whose identity gradually became submerged within the Mongol nation.[1] Genghis Khan's tribal totem became the national symbol of the Mongol coalition. It was constructed of the shoulder blades of a yak, from which hung nine white yak tails. From a distance, the Mongol standard looked like a Greek cross. When reports reached Europe of a great king who was making war on the Muslims far to the east, the similarity of the Mongol standard to the Greek cross of the Christians was taken as proof that the great king was a Christian warrior sent by God to destroy the Muslim infidels.

The structure of the Mongol army is usually attributed to the organizational genius of Genghis Khan himself. After uniting the steppe clans under his military and political leadership in 1206 C.E., he formally organized a national army based on the decimal system. The decimal system of military organization was not Genghis' invention, but the traditional way that tribal armies, including the armies of the Mongol tribe, had always been organized for war. It was Genghis' use of the decimal system to create a truly national army, in which assignment to combat command was based on competence rather than tribal loyalties, that was truly revolutionary. However, by the time the armies were reorganized in 1206, it is clear that the military intellect of Subotai was already well recognized by the Khan. It is at least likely that it was Subotai who influenced the Khan's thinking on how to reorganize the army. Genghis already had plans for the conquest of the Chin empire to the south, in China, and it must have been clear to Subotai and others that the army that fought and conquered the Mongolian tribes was poorly organized to attack and defeat such a major enemy. Organized as 1,000-man regiments, or *mingans*, its units lacked combat striking power on a strategic scale. The solution was to create the *touman*, an independent task force of 10,000 men capable of sustained operations over long distances. A unit this large had never before existed in Mongol history. The touman itself was to be part of even larger armies, and this required new levels of combat command and control. And so the new rank of *orlok* (literally, eagle, and technically equivalent to a field marshal) was created.[2] That Jebe and Subotai were appointed as the first field marshals speaks to the proposition that it may have been Subotai himself, and not Genghis Khan, who was the intellectual father of the new Mongol military reorganization.

Figure 2.1 portrays the table of organization of the Mongol army.[3] The smallest unit was a troop of ten soldiers called an *arban*, under the command of an officer called a *bagatur*. Ten arbans made up a squadron of 100 called a

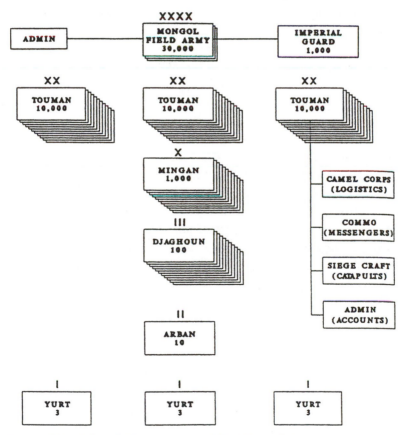

Figure 2.1   Table of Organization of the Mongol Army

djaghoun, and ten djaghouns composed a unit of 1,000, or a mingan. Ten mingans constituted the largest Mongol operational combat unit, the touman, consisting of 10,000 men.[4] A Mongol field army would typically be two or three toumans in strength, but could be tailored to any size. In the early days of the national army, officers were elected no doubt as a concession to tribal loyalty. But as the army became larger and more complex, election to command was retained only at the arban, or lowest, level, whereas command at the higher levels was appointed based on demonstrated excellence in battle. Transfers between units were forbidden, and soldiers served their entire lives in a single unit. As in the Roman Army, this practice did much to enhance unit morale and combat cohesion.

The army was almost entirely composed of cavalry, with forty percent heavy cavalry, and the remaining sixty percent designated light cavalry. There were no organic Mongol infantry units, but often units of conquered peoples (or even their civilian populations) were pressed into military service for specific campaigns. These units were regarded as completely expendable. It was common Mongol practice to attack the outlying and less defended cities and towns before bringing a major city or fortress under attack. The captured populations of these towns were then driven forward in advance of the Mongol army and forced directly against the enemy army. Often these "infantry" were used as laborers in sieges, or driven against the walls of a city where they suffered terrible casualties at the hands of the defenders. Sometimes, captured soldiers whose leaders vouched for their loyalty were used as garrison soldiers or guards for the supply train. For the most part, however, infantry played only a small role in Mongol tactics.

Most of what we know of the Mongol armies comes from the commentaries of their enemies. In order to explain their defeats at the hands of the Mongols, it became commonplace for Western commentators to exaggerate the size of Mongol armies. In fact, however, the Mongol armies were comparatively small for their time. During the *kurultai* meeting of the clans in 1206 C.E., the size of the army recorded in the *Secret History of the Mongols* was only 105,000 men. By 1227 C.E., according to Persian sources, the Mongol army had grown to only 129,000 men.[5] As Napoleon once remarked, "in war, quantity conveys a quality all its own." In almost every campaign, Mongol armies were smaller than the armies of their enemies were. It was Mongol cleverness that made them appear larger. Mongol armies moved with three remounts for each soldier in their train. Mongol commanders sometimes brought these remounts forward to march with the main body and set straw-dummies atop the remounts. At times, civilian captives were strapped to the horses. If captured members of the "infantry" were driven in front, the Mongol army would appear to be very much larger than it was. So, for example, a Mongol touman composed of 10,000 soldiers with straw dummies atop its normal complement of 30,000 remounts, and, say, 10,000 captured civilians driven before it as "infantry" would easily appear to be an army of 50,000 men, five times as large as it really was. The Mongol habit of using advanced agents, often recruited from the captured population, to spread rumors before a campaign that exaggerated the size of the army aided the deception and probably contributed to the propensity of the Mongol's enemies to greatly overestimate the size of the Khan's armies.

Manpower replenishment during the tribal wars was usually not a problem since it was the Mongol practice for defeated clans to abandon their former loyalties and make out as best they could with the new. Rarely did the defeated fight to the death, although with little to look forward to but execution, their leaders often did. The new Mongol armies were expected to remain in the field for years on end, and even victorious armies suffer casualties, which, along with disease and injury, take their inevitable toll—*wastage* in the British staff argot of World War I—on military manpower. Mongol armies quickly learned to make use of former enemies. To be sure, most of the civilian captives were killed or turned to infantry, at least for the moment. Those among them with particular skills, most importantly the metal smiths, were either sent back to Mongolia or distributed to the combat or logistic units. Engineers and those skilled in fabricating and utilizing siege machinery were also pressed into service. But by far the most use made of captured soldiers, especially those who were already trained as horse-borne bow warriors, was to incorporate them into the Mongol force itself.

As luck would have it, many of the peoples that came under the Mongol yoke as it drove west were tribal peoples whose method of warfare made common use of the horse and bow. Under the watchful eyes of Mongol officers whose harsh discipline could inflict instant death for disobedience or disloyalty, the Mongol armies often replenished their ranks during their long campaigns with captured enemy soldiers. Mongol commanders were not above striking temporary alliances with the warrior tribes in their path, and at times hired whole armies to their service. Fearing to leave potentially hostile forces in their wake once the campaign was over, however, the Mongols often turned on their new tribal allies and exterminated them to a man!

The raw material from which the Mongol soldier was forged made it possible to produce an excellent combat soldier. Mongols learned to ride at the age of three, taught not by their fathers but by their mothers. At age five, the child was given a bow. From then on, the Mongol male spent almost his entire life on horseback. The harsh environment of the Mongolian steppe, with its extremes of temperature, strong winds, limited water, and scarce game, accustomed the Mongolian horseman to hardship.[6] The Mongols were a naturally strong people with good eyesight and excellent visual memory. It was reported by travelers of the time that a Mongol soldier could distinguish between a man and animal across the Mongolian plain at a distance of up to four miles! The nomadic life equipped the soldier with a good knowledge of climatic conditions, water supply, and vegetation. Marco Polo reported that he had seen Mongol herdsmen go ten days without cooked food, subsisting on the blood drawn from the neck veins of their horses. The Mongol soldier routinely slept in the saddle and, with his remounts, was capable of movement over great distances without rest. In 1221 C.E., for example, the army of Genghis Khan covered 130 miles in two days without stopping for food. In 1241 C.E., Subotai moved his army toward the city of Pest, in Hungary, covering 180 miles in three days through snow, again without stopping for nourishment. The nomadic way of life made the Mongol a natural soldier. When coupled with the discipline and training of their military system, the Mongols became the most feared warriors in history—the Devil's Horsemen.

Tribal loyalties could be reduced somewhat by submerging the membership of the various tribes within the larger national military organization. A true sense of national identity required a new code of Mongol behavior, and Genghis Khan devised just such a code, the *Yassak*. The Mongol tribes had fought one another for centuries. The practice of taking slaves and conducting cattle and horse raids against each other engendered fierce conflict. Moreover, Mongols were polygamous, but traditional values forbade marriage to a member of one's own clan. This forced males to kidnap wives from other tribes, creating more opportunity for internecine warfare. Genghis Khan forbade all of these practices among the united tribes, and enforced a new code with strict military discipline. The code provided a number of penalties for specific crimes, including execution for cowardice in battle.[7] A favorite Mongol saying in this regard was, "He who does not obey the Yassak loses his head." The Yassak worked to bind the Mongol tribes together, because it had credibility in practice. In one case, a general officer named

Tuguchar, a son-in-law of Genghis Khan's, failed to execute his orders properly during the Khwarizmian campaign. He was summarily removed from his command, reduced to the rank of a common soldier, and lived the rest of his life as a soldier in the ranks until he died fighting in battle. The Yassak was a harsh military code, but it was applied equally across all social stations.

The most senior officers of the Mongol army were called orloks, equivalent to field marshals "who lead armies as large as they can gather,"[8] and were the most proven field commanders of the army. These senior commanders were selected strictly based on experience and proven ability. Jebe Noyan was a dashing, personally courageous commander with the heart of a gambler when it came to risky stratagems. He had fought against Genghis in the early days, and had proven his physical courage repeatedly in the tribal wars. Subotai, on the other hand, although having fought in command of small units during the tribal wars, seems to have been chosen for senior command primarily on the basis of his intellectual acumen in military matters. By the time of his promotion along with Jebe as one of the first two orloks selected personally by Genghis Khan, it seems likely that Subotai had been Genghis Khan's chief military strategist for many years. The practice of selecting only the most competent officers for combat command and only the very best for higher command was evident in the Mongol habit, even in the early days, of choosing competent officers even from outside of Genghis' tribe. Thus, of Genghis' "Four Dogs," none were of the Borjigin Mongols to whom Genghis belonged. Jelme and Subotai were both Uriangkhai, Khubilai was of royal lineage of another tribe, and Jebe was a Tayichigud. Later, there were Chinese, Muslim, and even an Englishman who held important positions in the Mongol armies. The selection of combat leadership, especially at the senior levels, on the basis of proven military excellence provided the Mongol army with the best generals of its day, officers that rarely failed to defeat their Muslim, Chinese, and/or Western counterparts.

The equipment of the Mongol soldier was simple, rugged, and, in the hands of the trained steppe cavalryman, deadly. The soldier wore either a brown or a blue tunic, the *kalat*, made of cotton or, in the winter, of fur. Thick leather boots with felt liners for the winter were standard issue. Given the reliance of the Mongols upon the horse and stirrup, it is curious that these boots had no heels. On top of the kalat, the heavy cavalry wore a coat of mail armor with a cuirass of ox-hide or metal scales covered in lacquered strips of leather. Light cavalry wore only the kalat and the lacquered armor, or a quilted kalat with no armor at all.[9] We know little about Mongol equipment prior to Genghis Khan. It is probable that when the various tribes were unified, those tribes that had served as mercenaries for the Chinese may have brought with them the superior weapons and armor of the Chinese. Metal-scale armor and chain mail were introduced to the Mongol armies only after their wars with the Chinese and the West. Certainly the Mongols learned the secret of making arrow and lance heads out of metal quite late, and it was only after Genghis' rise to power that the traditional materials of fire-hardened wood, bone, and horn were replaced by metal as military weapons stores.

After the first war with the Hsi-Hsia (1207), Genghis adopted the silk undershirt for his troops. This was an important innovation, somewhat comparable to the introduction of the flak jacket in modern armies. An arrow striking a solider would not pierce the silk undershirt. The twisting motion of the arrow wrapped the arrowhead around the silk and drove the material into the wound. Besides slowing the missile's penetration and reducing the severity of the wound, the silk made it much easier to extract the arrow from the body by pulling on the silk undershirt. Otherwise, pulling the arrow out by the shaft or pushing it through the body produced horrible wounds and increased fatalities. Had the Mongols practiced even a rudimentary degree of personal hygiene, it is possible that the silk undershirt would have done much to reduce infection as well. As things were, however, the Mongols rarely washed, and it was common for the undershirt to be replaced only after most of it had rotted away on the soldier's body.

On the march the Mongol soldier wore the traditional brimmed felt and leather hat with earflaps for protection against the cold wind. In battle, however, the soldier wore a casque helmet of leather, although some were made of iron later on. Leather or cloth draped from the rear rim in Persian fashion provided some protection for the neck. It is likely that some type of wool cap was worn underneath, and, perhaps, even a chinstrap was used to hold the helmet in place at the gallop. Ribbons and fur trim around the brim sometimes denoted rank. Figure 2.2 depicts the headgear and equipment of the Mongol heavy cavalryman. Mongol heavy cavalry sometimes carried a small, round wicker shield covered with leather to use with the lance. Light cavalry was composed of horse-archers, and the shield was not regularly used, as it interfered with the bow. Figure 2.3 portrays the Mongol light cavalryman and his equipment.

Heavy cavalry used the twelve-foot lance with a hook at the base of the blade for pulling adversaries off their horses. Alls Mongol cavalry carried two

Figure 2.2   Mongol Heavy Cavalryman

bows, one for short range and one for long-range firing, with at least two quivers of thirty arrows for a basic combat load of sixty arrows. Arrows varied by length of shaft, weight as a determinant of range, and type of arrowhead. While the arrows of the early armies were fashioned from fire-hardened wood, some arrows had tempered iron tips for piercing metal armor. Fire arrows and whistling signal arrows were also used.[10] All Mongol soldiers carried the lasso and a small dagger. Heavy cavalry also carried the curved scimitar, probably adopted from the Muslim armies, and a socketed battle-axe or mace, both probably adopted from the armies of the West. Some Mongol weapons are portrayed in Figure 2.4. Mongol troopers carried spare clothes in a leather saddlebag along with fishing line, a cooking pot, field rations, two leather canteens, files for sharpening arrowheads, and needle and thread. The Mongol saddlebag was somewhat water-resistant and was often tied to

Figure 2.3   Mongol Light Cavalryman

the tail of the horse when fording rivers. Another technique was to put all of one's kit in the saddlebag, and then trapping air within it while sealing the opening tightly. Folded and tied into a circle roll, the saddlebag could be used as a flotation device upon which the Mongol soldier could lie or sit while holding on to the tail of his horse as it swam across the river.

The bow was the basic weapon of the light cavalry. It was a small reflex composite bow constructed of layers of horn and sinew laminated over a wooden frame. It was highly lacquered to prevent moisture from delaminating the layers and was often carried in a case strapped to the side of the horse. With a pull of 160 pounds, the Mongol bow had a maximum range of about 300 hundred yards. This type of bow was rarely pulled to maximum power, however. The more common technique was to pull the bowstring rapidly back only a short distance and then release it in a snapping motion. The

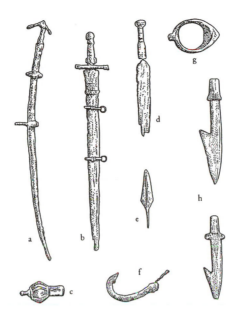

Weapons and gear from the territory of the Golden Horde; a and b, sabre and sword of uncertain provenance; c, iron spear-butt; d, bone sword-hilt; e, arrow-head; f, iron fish-hook; g, bronze ring for stringing bows; h, bone harpoons

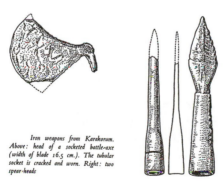

Iron weapons from Karakorum. Above: head of a socketed battle-axe (width of blade 16.5 cm.). The tubular socket is cracked and worn. Right: two spear-heads

Figure 2.4   Mongol Weapons

Mongols used a stone ring on the right thumb for grasping the bowstring that made this firing technique work acceptably well. The Mongol light cavalry were among the best horse-archers in the world, and were trained to release their arrows when the hooves of the horse were all simultaneously off the ground. This prevented the shock of the hooves striking the ground from throwing off the cavalryman's aim.

The Mongols rode Przhevalsky horses. This breed averaged thirteen to fourteen hands high, had thick legs, and was considerably shorter and less powerful than the warhorses of medieval Europe that carried the armored knights. This Mongol horse naturally used its hooves to scrape away snow from the tundra to reach grass or lichen underneath, and it even ate leaves from trees.[11] The animals' ability to forage in snow made it possible for the Mongols to use their ponies in severe winter conditions. In one campaign, for example, Mongol armies crossed the Pamir Mountains in the dead of winter! Besides his primary mount, the Mongol soldier always traveled with three additional horses to use as remounts. During a forced march, mounts were rotated quickly after only a few hours riding to husband the strength of the animal, a technique that extended the effective carrying range of each animal. Mongol cavalry rode mostly mares, from which they could obtain milk and blood for food. The soldier trained his mounts to follow along behind him like dogs and even to respond to calls and whistles. This permitted large numbers of horses to move with the army without large numbers of attendants to herd and feed them. The horse came to occupy an almost mystical place in Mongol society, and Genghis Khan issued strict regulations governing the humane treatment of horses. A horse ridden in battle, for example, was never killed for food but after his useful life, put out to pasture.

The normal "iron rations" of the Mongol soldier consisted of ten pounds of dried, powdered milk curd, millet meal, and two liters of *kumis*, a powerful alcoholic drink made from fermented mare's milk and blood. Meat was carried under the saddle, where the heat, sweat, and movement of the horse both cured and tenderized it. At the halt, Mongol soldiers would sometimes slice a piece of this jerky-like cured meat from under the saddle for a quick snack. Witnessing this, some foreign chroniclers recorded that the Mongols actually ate meat cut from their live horses![12] The dried milk curd was mixed with water and shaken in one of the two canteens to yield a loose yogurt. Herds of sheep, goats, yaks, and other domestic animals followed behind in the army's supply train. Apart from what the army could plunder from the vanquished, the Mongol soldier ate almost anything, including rats, lice, and even the afterbirth of foaled mares. Their habit of consuming raw intestines from freshly killed game, squeezing out the fecal material as they went, particularly outraged Muslims.

The individual soldier could be trained within his unit to sharpen his natural skills derived from nomadic life. Training the army to act in unison and to respond to command was another matter. The Mongols trained their armies in the *nerge*, the great animal hunt held at the beginning of each winter. The hunt lasted for three months, and involved the entire army assembled in full battle dress. The army was assembled along a line almost eighty miles long. At the command of the Great Khan, the army moved forward, driving before it all living things. The end of the hunt was hundreds of miles away. As the army moved doggedly ahead, the wings of the army gradually extended out to form a semicircle. Day after day, the game was driven ahead and contained within the slowly closing circle. Eventually, the circle was closed, and contracted tighter and tighter, driving the game toward the center. The soldiers acted in concert as units to prevent any game, even the smallest rabbit, from escaping the circle. If an animal slipped past a soldier, he and his officer were punished. As the circle tightened, the teeming game within it tried desperately to escape against the efforts of the soldiers to contain it. Then the killing began, and the soldiers dismounted and attacked the game, with the goal of killing everything within the circle! The bears, tigers, wolves, and other large animals struck out in terror, and hand-to-hand engagements between animal and man occurred. The area where the killing was done, or the *gerka*, ran red with blood, until, at the request of the tribal elders, the Great Khan put a stop to the killing.[13] The hunt was excellent practice, in that it trained the army to operate in concert while providing the leadership of the smaller combat units with an excellent opportunity to know and direct their troops in a difficult task, under very difficult conditions, indeed.

The Mongol army attempted to institutionalize excellence in command and staff assignments by establishing the Imperial Guard, or *keshig*. In the early days, the Guard had comprised only 1,000 men and consisted of the Khan's household, personal servants, and old, trusted comrades from the tribal wars who acted as a battle guard when engaged. The Imperial Guard originally came from the personal bodyguard of the Khan, and this was reflected in the names of the three guard units that composed it. There was the *tunghaut*, or Day Guard, the *kabtaut*, or Night Guard, and the Quiver Bearers, or battle guard. Genghis Khan formed the keshig in 1206, when he reorganized the army to make it capable of large-scale, sustained military operations against more powerful opponents. The *Secret History* tells us that the original guard was increased to 10,000 men and that it was commanded by an officer named Nayaga. Somewhat later, and here we may reasonably suspect the influence of Subotai, more the military intellectual than combat commander, the keshig had become the Mongol equivalent of a staff and command college for combat commanders and military strategists.[14]

The Imperial Guard became the home of the best, brightest, and most promising of the Mongol army's military commanders and staff officers. The candidates for membership in the keshig were identified early in their careers and selected because of outstanding performance in lower level command and by an annual competition among all the outstanding men in the army. Selection was strictly on merit. While some were granted membership because they were the sons of important nobility, those who failed to meet standards of proficiency were quickly weeded out, as in the aforementioned case involving the son-in-law of Genghis Khan himself. Every officer in the keshig was trained in staff work and attended education and briefing sessions. After the Chinese wars, great emphasis was placed on the employment of siege machinery. Any officer of the Imperial Guard was presumed to be able to command a touman at a moment's notice if events required (an expectation that, like Napoleon's order requiring all junior officers to carry a field marshal's baton in their knapsacks in case they had to assume command of the army, was not met very much in practice). On the battlefield, the commands of a guardsman took precedence over those of the commander of any unit of mingan or below.

The Imperial Guard was regarded as the best fighting touman in the army and took its place next to the Great Khan in the center of the line, to be employed at his command. Once more, Napoleon's practice of using his Imperial Guard the same way is striking. Each of the three mingans in the imperial touman had differently colored uniforms and horses for the Day Guard, Night Guard, and Quiver Bearers. The remaining seven mingans constituted the old elite life guards who fought with Genghis during the tribal wars and protected his person. Subotai seems to have served with the life guards early in his career, if only for a short time, and used the title of bagatur awarded to all guardsmen to the end of his life even though he carried higher rank. The title means "knight", but it also means "the valiant." The life guards wore black kalats and armor trimmed in red. Each guardsman rode a black horse with a red leather harness and saddle.

The exact structure of the Mongol staff organization is not certain, and it is not possible to reconstruct it in detail. However, it is noted in several sources that the Khan's military staff was comprised of eleven senior staff officers, each one probably in charge of a specific staff section. It is certain that the army staff was located within the Imperial Guard, and it is likely that each touman had smaller, but similar, staff sections within its administrative staff structure. The general staff had sections dealing with medical support, and it is well known that the Mongol armies were equipped with units of Chinese, Indian, and Muslim medical practitioners. A mobile diplomatic corps was part of the staff for use in the conduct of negotiations. Units of interpreters were evident, as were scribes and record keepers, an interesting innovation for a people that were completely illiterate until the Uighurs provided them with an alphabet and a method of writing. An extensive intelligence apparatus, including sections that collected and analyzed strategic intelligence, was adopted and incorporated from the Chinese, as were field agents, mapmakers, and surveyors. The Mongol intelligence officers counted and recorded everything, and an accurate body count was an essential part of any Mongol after-action report. At the battle of Liegnitz, special squads roamed the battlefield after the fight and systematically cut off the right ear of every slain enemy soldier, collecting them in nine sacks for presentation to the commander. Horrible as such mutilation is, the practice provided the Mongol intelligence officers with an accurate body count.[15]

At the end of the day's march, the Mongols always pitched their camps facing south. Each wing of the army encamped in the same location relative to the center of the army, called the *khol*, or Middle Army. The Army of the Left (*junghar*) always faced east, while the Army of the Right (*baraunghar*) always faced west. When encamped, officers called *yurtchis* (after *yurt*, meaning "dwelling") served as the equivalent of modern quartermasters.[16] These officers chose the campsites, organized the flow of supplies, and established and operated communications. The highest-ranking yurtchis were responsible for conducting reconnaissance and intelligence gathering. Within the camp, Chinese, Indian, and Persian physicians set up their dressing stations to treat the sick and wounded. Regular inspections of men and equipment were conducted, and the punishment for failing to keep equipment in good condition was severe. An extremely important function of the yurtchis was the care and operation of the army's camel corps, upon which it relied heavily for its supplies. While it is well known that the Mongols were great horse breeders, it is often overlooked that they were also successful camel breeders. The Mongol armies were frequently supplied by large corps of camels shuffling between supply points and the army. Figure 2.5 portrays a Mongol field army on the march.

Among the more important staff officers and specialists were those in the Imperial Guard who dealt with siegecraft and artillery. During the first war against the Chinese, the Mongols quickly discovered that they were powerless to subdue cities. Accordingly, as they gained victory in China they

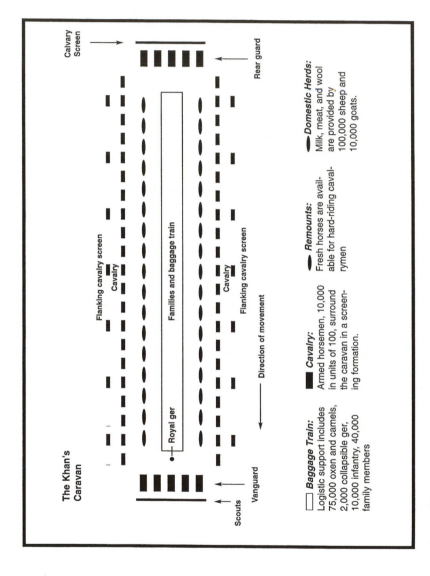

Figure 2.5   Mongol Field Army on the March

incorporated Chinese siege specialists and siege engines into their armies. Later, the Mongol army had a special corps of Persian engineers and siege experts within it. The army had a standing order to spare these experts in rival armies whenever a city was captured. From the use of siege engines, the Mongols gradually developed field artillery. Mongol siege engines included light and heavy catapults to launch all sorts of missiles against cities and fortifications. In one case, Mongol artillerymen cut down mulberry trees and soaked the logs in water to give them weight. The logs were then cut into smaller pieces and fired at the city-walls. Ballistae-like giant crossbows were also used, as was a variation of the European trebuchet in later years. These same machines were employed as artillery, shooting fireworks to confuse the enemy. Clay pots full of incendiary materials fired by timed wicks, naphtha pots, and projectiles called a *duyao yanqiu,* or a "poison-and-smoke ball," made of sulphur, nitre, aconite, oil charcoal, resin, and wax, were fired by these catapults.[17] The use of artillery was closely integrated into Mongol tactics, even against field armies deployed in the open, rather than behind defensive walls. At the battle of the Sajo River the Mongols opened the attack with an artillery bombardment. Some of the Mongol siege engines are portrayed in Figure 2.6.

Chinese and Saracen siege-engines as used by the Mongols : ballistae for throwing heavy stones and other massive missiles

Figure 2.6   Mongol Siege Machinery

Mechanical sophistication in siege operations never blinded the Mongols to the use of more primitive, but effective, means of assaulting cities. During the siege of Gurganj, the capital of Kazrem, thousands of local citizens were herded together for the final assault on the walls and driven by the Mongols into the city's moat. The defenders slaughtered their own countrymen in the thousands until the moat was filled with corpses upon which a ramp was constructed to assault the walls. The Mongols were capable of incredible cruelty, but their cruelty always served some military or political objective.

Mongol expertise in the military operational arts always functioned within the context of a larger political strategy of which military operations were but a part. This subordination of military to political objectives was clearly evident in the extensive preparations that preceded any Mongol military campaign. Sometimes these preparations required more than a year to complete. The Imperial Guard, for example, had a permanent and extensive intelligence section that dealt with political and strategic intelligence. They maintained up-to-date records on all major nations and provided written records and briefings to the military commanders. Political intelligence was regarded by the Mongols as the most important, and they were particularly interested in any personal rivalries among the enemy leadership that could be exploited during the campaign. The Mongol attack on Hungary, for example, was predicated on the assumption that the intense rivalry between the Germans and the Papacy would prevent any unified effort against the Mongol invasion. The Mongols also correctly assessed that the petty rivalries of Russian and Polish princes would preclude any national military effort against the Mongol forces. Mongol preparations for war always centered upon a strategic assessment of the enemy, including its ability to mount and sustain a successful coalition of forces and maintain the will to fight. Mongol intelligence officers were far more than "arrow counters."

Extensive psychological warfare efforts preceded a Mongol campaign, with different themes directed at diverse target audiences. Merchants and spies spread rumors; the wealthy were told that under the Mongols trade would prosper, while the poor were told that they would be liberated from their oppression and that a just law would govern their lives. Deliberate rumors exaggerating the size of the Mongol armies were sowed. Behind all of it was the Mongol threat of cruelty and devastation; facts that needed little in the way of psychological explanation to make them credible. Preparation for war required that the campaigns be timed correctly to take maximum advantage of terrain, weather, and food supplies. Mongols always chose the season of the attack with great care. Iraq was invaded in the spring of 1258, a time when the heat was less severe and malaria not a danger. The Russian campaign of 1237–1238 was timed for the winter, when the rivers and marshes were frozen and the entire theater of operations resembled a vast, snow-covered Mongolian plain.

The strength of the Mongol army lay in its ability to conduct combat operations with an efficiency and effectiveness that far surpassed the abilities of their enemies to resist. The Mongols seem to have been the first army to conceive of military command in a manner that stressed objectives while leaving the choice of ways and means to the unit commander, a theory of tactical application and control that the Germans later called *Auftragstaktik*. Unit commanders were briefed on the general operational plan, and objectives were specified for each touman. Within these broad guidelines, the field commander was afforded the widest possible latitude in accomplishing the objectives. Stress was placed on initiative, innovation, and flexibility of execution.

The Mongol army advanced into enemy territory in large columns widely separated from each other. Command and control between the columns was maintained by units of courier riders moving constantly between the columns. The tactical communication system of couriers also used semaphore-like signals and even lanterns to send messages. This ability to communicate regularly, even daily, made it possible for the army commander to exercise command and control over the entire army even though it was widely dispersed. Each column was preceded by screens of cavalry scouts that acted as reconnaissance units, sometimes deployed as many as seventy miles to the front of the main column. Similar units were deployed on the flanks and to the rear of the army as it marched.[18] The operational principle was for the army to move divided while attempting to find the enemy. Once the enemy was located, light reconnaissance units could be used to fix it in place while the larger columns concentrated rapidly, striking the enemy at the decisive time and place or from a number of directions at once. The Mongol approach to contact represented a perfect application of the old dictum, "march divided, fight united."

Once contact was made and the decision to engage the main force taken, the touman advanced into battle in five single lines. Each line was tightly packed to maximize the shock of impact, but the lines themselves were separated by a considerable distance, sometimes two hundred yards. The first two were composed of heavy cavalry, followed by three lines of light cavalry. As the lines closed with the enemy, the first line of light cavalry broke into a gallop and rode through the gaps in the lines of heavy cavalry to its front and engaged the enemy with volleys of arrow fire. At the same time, the rear ranks of light cavalry fired volleys over the heads of the heavy cavalry. As the first rank of light cavalry closed with the enemy, it rode obliquely across the front firing as it went. If the timing was right—and it usually was—just as the rate of arrow fire from the light cavalry reached its height, the light cavalry broke off and the heavy cavalry was upon the enemy in force, engaging it with maximum shock value.[19]

In set-piece battle, the first engagements were always carried out by the light cavalry, horse archers whose task it was to lay down a heavy field of "fire" to inflict as many casualties as possible prior to engagement by the heavy cavalry. European and Chinese armies relied almost entirely upon shock delivered by heavy cavalry and infantry. The Mongol horse archer attack was designed to considerably weaken the enemy force prior to the main engagement. Again and again, Mongol light cavalry would swoop down and around the packed enemy force firing into the ranks as it went. If the enemy retained its discipline and remained in place, the horse archers kept attacking until the casualty rate was so high as to render the enemy force ineffective. If the enemy attacked the Mongol archers, they would conduct an orderly and phased retreat firing backwards from their horses as they went until the pursuing enemy could be taken in the flank or head-on by the waiting Mongol heavy cavalry. As Di Plano Carpini noted in his book, the Mongol light cavalry "wounded and killed men and horses, and only when the men and horses are worn down by the arrows, do they come to close quarters." Sir Basil H. Liddell-Hart notes that this technique "is the first time in military history that 'fire' is employed systematically to pave the way for the assault."[20]

If the light cavalry failed to open the enemy front, the Mongols might execute a maneuver called the *tulughama* or standard sweep (Figure 2.7). While the heavy cavalry engaged the enemy from the front, the light cavalry sent a wing around the entire formation to engage the enemy on the flank. Sometimes the light cavalry might ride entirely around the battlefield and strike the enemy from the rear. The idea was to strike the enemy from at least two directions, confuse him, break his ranks, and then drive home the attack with the last line of heavy cavalry.[21]

The charge of the heavy cavalry was always the main player in the endgame of a Mongol attack. All battlefield maneuvers prior to the actual charge were carried out in complete silence with the horses moving at the speed of a "wolf-lope." Units were controlled by flags, colored lanterns, and hand sig-

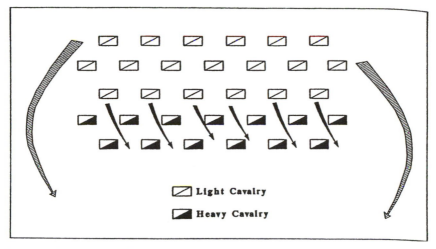

Figure 2.7   Mongol *Tulughama* Maneuver

nals. At the time of the attack, this silence was broken by the sound of the *naccara*, the great kettledrum that sounded the beat and tempo of the attack. The silence was suddenly shattered by hideous yells and screams as the Mongols attempted to psychologically shatter the nerve of their enemy.

Another Mongol tactic was the *mangudai*, in which a unit of light cavalry rode directly at the enemy center engaging in a hopeless attack. After some initial combat, and on signal, the horsemen would feign panic, break ranks, ride through their own formations, and turn and run in what seemed a disorganized manner. The idea was to entice the enemy to follow in force, something that European armies of mounted knights seeking individual glory often found irresistible. During a chase of a mile or two sufficient to allow the pursuing enemy force to lose cohesion and scatter, the Mongols waited in ambush on the flank. Suddenly, from out of the concealment, came a hail of arrows followed rapidly by the charge of heavy cavalry on rested horses. Within minutes, the enemy was surrounded. Mongol archers shot the horses out from underneath the enemy horsemen. On foot, the European or Muslim knights were easy prey to Mongol lancers or archers. Often, as at the battle of Liegnitz, the slaughter was horrendous. Mongol cavalry also fought in staggered formations or in open or closed files depending upon the circumstances.

The Mongols were experts at pursuit. Their tactical doctrine defined victory as nothing less than the annihilation of the enemy army. Once the enemy had been driven from the field, the Mongols sometimes pursued for weeks, until almost every enemy soldier was slain or captured. Following an old practice of the tribal wars, Mongol commanders often ordered the pursuit of defeated enemy rivals to their death. In both the Khwarizmian and European campaigns, the Mongols sent special task forces to track down and capture the enemy commanders. Operating as it usually did, at the end of long supply lines, no Mongol field army could risk leaving the remnants of an enemy army to reform and fight again and threaten their supply lines. Along with a ruthless pursuit, the Mongols would sometimes devastate the surrounding countryside. In 1299 C.E., for example, the Mongols defeated the Mamlukes at Salaamiyet. Mongol units were recorded as pursuing the remnants of the enemy army as far as Gaza—300 miles from the battlefield!

The speed of movement of the Mongol armies was among its greatest combat capabilities, and it was a common occurrence for a Mongol touman to move hundreds of miles in a few days appearing suddenly behind the enemy army or at the gates of some fortified city deep in the enemy rear. Speed was one reason why Mongol commanders like Jebe and Subotai could take such great risks in maneuvering their forces. Given the best of circumstances, it was almost impossible for a European or Chinese army to ambush or take a Mongol touman by surprise. In the event that a Mongol commander found himself hard-pressed, the ability of his army to move quickly meant that it could almost always retreat faster than the enemy could pursue.

Genghis Khan is supposed to have been told by a captured Chinese officer that while the Mongols had captured an empire on horseback, the empire could not be ruled from horseback. Genghis Khan bequeathed an empire to his son, Ogedai, who then had to govern it. Across such a far-flung realm as the Mongol empire, government was impossible without sound communications. In 1234 C.E., Ogedai Khan formalized the establishment of an imperial communication system called the *yam*. This was a system of horse-and-rider stations at fixed intervals of twenty-five miles (so Marco Polo tells us) across the entire length and breadth of the empire. Riders could be strapped in their saddles to ride throughout the night while the horse found its way to the next station as the rider slept. To reduce the time between changes of mounts, the messengers sometimes wore bells to warn the station attendants of their approach in time to prepare the fresh mount. The responsibility for staffing and operating the yam was given to the army, and communications stations were now routinely established in the wake of the army on the move. The yam also functioned as an efficient tactical and strategic communication system.[22]

3 THE WARS AGAINST THE CHIN

Having united Mongolia under a single standard, Genghis Khan and his generals began to contemplate the world around them. Map 3.1 portrays the geographical position of the new Mongolian realm relative to the locations of the major nations that threatened Mongolia itself or acted as barriers to further expansion. To the southeast lay the great colossus of China, safe behind the Great Wall, and divided into the rival kingdoms of the Chin and the Sung. Directly to the south was the Tangut kingdom of Hsi-Hsia and its powerful cavalry and infantry armies organized along Chinese lines. To the southwest lay the kingdom of the "western Liao" or Kara-Khitai (literally "Black Cathay") that stretched right across "the roof of the world" and the Pamir Mountains.

All four of these kingdoms had their origin in the motherland of ancient China, which had once been of such enormous size that its borders ran "from the regions of perpetual ice to the regions of perpetual summer."[1] Three centuries before the birth of Genghis Khan ancient China had broken into two great realms, the Sung empire to the south of the Yangtze River and the northern empire of the Liao Dynasty. The Liao lasted just two centuries before being replaced by the Chin (literally "gold") dynasty from which the modern name of China is derived. One of the powerful Liao princes refused to recognize the imperial authority of the upstart Chin and migrated northward with his followers where they imposed their rule upon a native Turcoman people and founded the kingdom of Kara-Khitai. Sometime earlier, the southern Sung had been forced to recognize the independence of the Tangut princes who once served as Chinese viceroys for the territories bordering on Tibet and the Gobi to the northwest. This was the powerful state of Hsi-Hsia.

Map 3.1   Mongolia and Surrounding States, 1206

By the time Genghis Khan had achieved mastery over Mongolia, ancient China had given birth to the four states that bordered the new Mongolian realm. Regardless of who ruled China, the Chinese had not usually been hostile to the Mongolian tribes that lived on their borders. It had been Chinese policy for centuries to pursue a policy of *i chi i*, literally, "use barbarians to control barbarians." To this end, China had successfully played off one tribe or coalition of tribes against another, shifting this way and that, always with the goal of forestalling the rise of a single coalition that could unite all the tribes under one banner. Genghis Khan himself, as well as his father, had served as allies of the Chinese in their conflicts with other tribes. After the war with the Tartars in 1198, Genghis had even been appointed a frontier vassal of the Chinese emperor in recognition of his military service to the crown. To be sure Genghis knew that several of his ancestors had met their deaths at the hands of the Chinese, but that had been long ago. As great a power as China was, it harbored no territorial ambitions in Mongolia. Why, then, did Genghis and his generals go to war against China?

The answer lies in the fact that the Mongols were a warrior society in which personal bravery in war defined one's social status. Even as organized under Genghis Khan, Mongol society was nothing more than a very large tribe. Its social institutions were little more than enlarged versions of tribal institutions and were not in any sense proper state institutions. And appropriately so, for Genghis Khan brought to the world no vision of a Mongol society other than what it was and always had been. There was no thought of building a different social order or, for that matter, of conquering and administering another state. This vision came much later, under Genghis' grandsons, and it was brought to the attention of the Mongol khans by Chinese and Muslim advisors. To Genghis and his generals war was a way of life, and the states that lay on Mongolia's borders were tempting targets for raids and plunder, splendid opportunities for Mongol warriors to do what they had always done, make war, carry off booty, and get drunk in their tents!

THE WARS AGAINST THE CHIN

Genghis' attack against the Chin touched off a war without end. Beginning in 1211, the wars raged on and off until Genghis' death (1227) and were continued in spurts by his son and successor, Ogedai, until Subotai put an end to it in 1234 after finally capturing the new Chin capitol at Kai-feng-fu (Nanking). In every campaign against the Chin, the Mongols were militarily successful, and in the long years of war lost only two battles. Despite victory after victory, the Mongols were unable to bring about a strategic decision. Such a prolonged war of successful campaigns leading to no strategic conclusion was surely not typical of earlier or later Mongol wars but can be explained in several ways. First, China was enormous, with a population of approximately 50,000,000 against a Mongolian population of, perhaps, 3,000,000 at the maximum. The invasion of China in 1211 amounted to a maximum military effort on the part of the Mongols that produced an army of 120,000 soldiers. Chinese field armies were enormous, and despite repeated defeats, could be raised and deployed again and again, whereas Mongol losses were much more difficult to replace, often relying upon defections of unit commanders formerly in the Chinese ranks. Under these conditions, whenever a Chinese army met its destruction, it was quickly replaced by another making it almost impossible for the Mongols to achieve a strategic decision on the battlefield.

Besides their great size, Chinese armies were formidable in their fighting capability. Composed of large, disciplined infantry phalanxes armed with pikes and equipped with armor, and substantial cavalry formations, Chinese armies were also well-led and, for the most part, sufficiently disciplined to maintain their composure under attack. These armies had excellent logistics capabilities, insofar as they were deployed in and amid a complex of forts and store cities across the country from which they could draw supplies and to which they could withdraw when things went badly. The Chinese system of defensive works made a land of swift and broad rivers, paddies, and dikes very difficult for the Mongols to turn to their advantage. The Chinese defense infrastructure consisted of the Great Wall itself, heavily fortified secondary walls behind it to canalize the enemy into movement in predictable directions, small and great fortresses deployed in depth, and fortified positions in the mountain passes. Some of the cities were impregnable. Peking (Chung-tu), for example, possessed walls of stamped clay that were forty feet high, replete with sloped battlements of brick with 900 battle towers, thirteen gates, and surrounded by three concentric moats. Connected to the main fortress by subterranean tunnels were four smaller fortress cities, each about a mile square and equipped with its own garrisons, arsenals, and stores. The main city counted a garrison of 20,000 men, while each of the four outer cities was manned by 4,000 more soldiers. The population of Chung-tu was about 1,000,000 souls that could be put to work in defense of the city.[2] Although the Mongols had encountered fixed fortifications in their brief war with Hsi-Hsia (1207–1210), their primitive siege capability was useless against the strongly fortified cities of the Chinese.[3]

In addition, the Mongol way of war was ill suited to dealing with the Chinese, because it was not a war of conquest and occupation but a war of raids and plunder. Even when the Mongols could storm a town and ravage it, they quickly withdrew with their booty, leaving the place without a garrison or occupied by only a token force. Under these circumstances, the Chinese easily reoccupied the town and rebuilt its fortifications. Even as the Mongol *toumans* advanced across China destroying everything in their path, the Chinese were often close behind, rebuilding the city walls, dams, dikes, and other fortifications and restocking them with civilians and soldiers. This had the effect of preserving a strategic, if not tactical, stalemate, which often blocked the Mongol avenue of retreat whenever they encountered an army to their front. In a number of cases, the Mongol generals had to recapture the same city or fortress several times.[4] Under these circumstances, the Chinese could prevent a strategic decision in favor of the Mongols.

Finally, the Mongol practice of wholesale massacre to inspire fear and cause disruption, as well as the practice of killing the defeated so that they could no longer contribute to the resistance (a habit that shook the West to its core later on), had only limited effect on the Chinese. With a population of 50,000,000 inhabitants from which to draw, there were always sufficient people to take the place of those slain. For years, the Mongols ravaged China but could not force it to its knees, even as many, many thousands were killed in the effort. The Mongols found themselves trapped in a war of attrition that they could not win. Map 3.2 portrays the various Mongol campaigns against the Chin between 1211 and 1214.

Before Genghis Khan could engage the Chinese, he had first to insure that he would not be attacked from the rear. To this end, he launched an attack against Hsi-Hsia in 1207. Two years before, the Mongols had raided a few border towns and burnt some frontier settlements. This was the Mongols' first encounter with fortified towns. They also encountered infantry arrayed in phalanxes of armored pikemen for the first time, the same kind of infantry they would eventually encounter in China.[5] We do not know how successful the Mongol cavalrymen were against the pike infantry in Hsi-Hsia, but on at least one occasion the infantry was able to hold its own in open country until a relief force of cavalry arrived and drove off the Mongols. It was in Hsi-Hsia that the Mongol armies first encountered two of the major elements of combat: infantry and fortifications. Except for the practice of the Mongol forest tribes to construct lagers of logs and branches to fight behind, the Mongol armies had no practical military experience in dealing with fortifications of any type. In addition, infantry was almost completely unknown in Mongolia, where all tribal armies were cavalry armies. It was during the war against Hsi-Hsia (1207–1210) that the Mongols gained some familiarity with both of these forms of combat, but in neither case was it extensive.

In 1207, Genghis Khan mounted a strong invasion of Hsi-Hsia to reduce the strength of its armies and the state to vassalage. In response, the western Liao sent an army of 50,000 to block the invader's path, only to see it defeated in a pitched battle. However, a second army quickly engaged the Mongols and succeeded in blocking the Mongol advance for more than two months. While details are lacking, this suggests at least that the Mongols had

Map 3.2   Mongol Campaigns in China, 1211–1215

some difficulty in dealing with the armored heavy infantry, while the cavalry was sufficiently disciplined to hold the field against the Mongol horsemen. The armies of Hsi-Hsia were organized along traditional Chinese lines and apparently demonstrated to the Mongol generals that disciplined infantry operating in concert with good cavalry could offset the Mongol advantages in speed, suppressive fire, and maneuver. The Mongols may well have taken the lesson to heart, for in their later campaigns against the Muslims and in the West, whenever an opposing army held its ground or could not be lured into a disastrous pursuit, the Mongols broke contact and moved on toward other objectives.

It was at one of the fortified towns of Hsi-Hsia, Volohai by name, that the Mongols received their first serious education in siege warfare. For weeks, the Mongol generals attacked the city in an attempt to take it by storm, only to suffer terrible casualties. Unable to take the city, Genghis resorted to a brilliant ruse that has become legend. He offered to lift the siege if the defenders would provide his men with 1,000 cats and 10,000 swallows. Although the defenders must have been puzzled, they nevertheless met the demand. Genghis then ordered his men to tie a tuft of wool to each of the cats and birds, light the tufts on fire, and turn the animals and birds loose. The cats ran for their lairs as the birds returned to their nests and within hours the city was ablaze! While the fire raged and occupied the defenders, the Mongols stormed the walls and took the city. The success at Volohai did not blind the Mongols to the fact that they were ill equipped to deal with fortifications, which China possessed in abundance.

The war with Hsi-Hsia ended in 1210 and Genghis summoned his commanders to a meeting in Mongolia. So important was this meeting that Genghis sent the following message to his commanders: "One who remains in his own locality instead of coming to me to receive my instructions will have the fate of a stone dropped in water . . . he will simply disappear."[6] Under the direction of his son Ogedai, Genghis ordered that his officers study the art of siegecraft, and directed that supplies of scaling ladders, sandbags, and large shields to protect the siegers be fashioned. Every tribe was now commanded to create a special section of men to learn siegecraft. Camel trains were introduced to move the equipment, and special arsenals were created. While this was an improvement in Mongol siege capability, in fact it was not a very large improvement. The Mongols still lacked any detailed knowledge of engineering and its role in siege operations and were completely unaware of the existence, let alone the application, of the sophisticated siege engines required to reduce the battlements of even medium-sized cities. Because the bridge, that staple of Chinese, Muslim, and Western land communication, was unknown in Mongolia, no Mongol had ever seen a moat, nor did they know how to cross one. Although the war with Hsi-Hsia taught the Mongols the rudiments of siege technique, it was so rudimentary as to be useless against the Chinese.

The accounts of the war against the Chin tell us little of the part played by Subotai in the fighting, and what we have comes from a single Chinese source. Still, it is worth noting that the Chinese chronicle refers to the brilliant Subotai who planned the attack and many of the follow-on operations. However, we cannot be certain of this. Genghis, after all, was still alive, and victory is always attributed to the commander. While more can be said, and with greater certainty, about Subotai's role in the war against the Khwarizm-Shah and, later, Russia and the West, we can be certain about Subotai's role in the Chin wars in only three instances. First, during the initial attack against the Chin Subotai commanded one of the toumans of the advanced guard that assaulted the Great Wall and later fought at the battle of Shansi. Second, when Mukhali was sent to bring the Khitans under control, it was Subotai who crossed Manchuria and attacked Korea. Third, between 1231 and 1233, Subotai assumed command of the Mongol armies in China and ended the war by the successful battle and eventual siege of Kai-feng-fu.

THE ASSAULT ON THE GREAT WALL

In 1211, Genghis assembled the Mongol army on the banks of the Kerulen River. Over 400 miles to the southeast, across the vast Gobi desert, lay the northern frontier of the Chin Empire, protected by the Great Wall. The Mongol army was the largest ever put into the field, numbering between 100,000 and 120,000 men. It was early spring, the time of the melting snows, and the route of advance across the Gobi now possessed adequate water and fodder for the huge supply and animal train that followed in the wake of the army. Far to the front of the advanced guard were the reconnaissance scouts who led the way. Anyone crossing their path was arrested and held—sometimes executed—for security was of the utmost importance. In the wake of the scouts came the *yurtchi*, the logistics officers whose task it was to select the locations of the night camps and to insure that adequate food and water supplies were provided. Behind the yurtchi came the toumans of the advanced guard marching widely apart but striking for the same target, the eastern salient of the Great Wall. Subotai, in command of the advance guard, commanded one touman while Mukhali and Jebe commanded the other two. Thirty thousand Mongol cavalrymen bore down on the Great Wall. The main army under Genghis himself, between 80,000 and 90,000 strong, trailed far behind, its route of advance and ultimate destination unknown to the Chin.

Ahead lay the land of the Chin and its capital, Peking, a formidable fortress on the vast plain between it and the Great Wall to the north. Inside the

Great Wall lay two additional walls, thirty to sixty miles apart, constructed along steep hills to take maximum advantage of the land's natural obstacles. Along the wall and behind it lay a vast system of fortresses constructed in such a way as to offer a coordinated defense of the capital. The Mongol advanced guard was detected in plenty of time by the Chin intelligence service as it advanced straight for the eastern wall. The Chin generals reacted predictably. Huge armies were quickly concentrated close to Peking itself while the forward fortresses, strong points, and wall garrisons were strengthened. With the trap set, the Chin waited for Subotai to attack the Great Wall. As if to fulfill their expectations, Subotai and his 30,000 men moved straight at them.

Then, from the west, came terrible news! Subotai's advance and demonstration against the Great Wall in the east had been a feint. While the main force of the Chin army was concentrated around the capital facing north, 120 miles further west Genghis and the main body of the Mongol army had crossed the Great Wall without firing a shot. This section of the wall was guarded not by Chinese troops, but by Onguts, ethnic relatives to the Mongols whom the Mongol intelligence service had cultivated for years as possible allies. Faced with the choice of remaining loyal to the Chin and having to do battle with a huge Mongol army or going over to the Mongols, the Onguts changed sides and allowed the Mongols to pass through the western battlements unhindered. Farther to the east, Subotai broke contact, pull back from the wall, and disappeared.

The Chinese generals had been caught badly out of position, and they moved quickly to deploy their armies westward, keeping themselves between the Mongol main force and the Chin capital. They began to move west to block the Mongol advance on Peking, but infantry can only move as fast as their feet can carry them. Although the Chin cavalry could move somewhat faster, their tactical doctrine required that they always maneuver with their infantry on the battlefield. Except for a few advanced reconnaissance units, the Chin army moved ponderously over the Chinese landscape, probing to make contact with Genghis' main army. Under these conditions, the choice of the battlefield fell to the Mongols, who chose the open plain where the passes through the Shansi Mountains debouched into the flatlands between the mountains and the border.

Genghis could easily have struck the Chinese army piecemeal as it made its way through the passes and entered upon the open plain unit by unit. Strangely, he permitted the Chin army to complete their march and form up for battle on the open plain. Deployed for battle, the Chin army was arranged in dense infantry formations supported on the wings by cavalry. One surmises the presence of heavy pike-infantry phalanxes, their soldiers protected by armor, helmets, and shields. Much of the remaining infantry, however, would have been conscript infantry, equipped with weapons but lacking armor and disciplined fighting skills. The cavalry was composed of heavily armored nobility mounted on sound horses, somewhat heavier in weight than the Mongols, but no match in terms of speed, maneuver, and firepower. The Chin armies probably outnumbered the Mongols, and Genghis' deployment on open ground seemed to give away the Mongol advantages of surprise and maneuver. It was to be a set-piece battle. The victory would belong to the side that held its ground and did the most killing.

It is likely that the Mongols struck first, with their waves of light cavalry passing boldly across the enemy front, firing volley after volley of arrows as each wave passed before the packed Chin infantry formations. While the heavy infantry probably fared better, the conscript infantry would have been decimated, with whole units dying where they stood or fleeing the field. The Mongols would now have launched their main attack with heavy cavalry engaging the enemy cavalry all across the line, but most desperately on the wings. The battle raged most of the morning, as the Chin held their ground against the Mongol frontal attack. Then, just before noon, Subotai and his three toumans struck the Chin armies simultaneously in both flanks and in the rear. Subotai's columns seemed to appear from out of nowhere. After the feint against the eastern wall, the Mongol advanced guard had broken contact with the defenders, withdrawn from the field, and disappeared. As the Chin armies marched at foot-speed to cover the 120 miles from the eastern wall to the battlefield, Subotai was crossing the Great Wall at the same place as Genghis' main force had crossed. Subotai and his three toumans had ridden the entire distance outside the perimeter of the wall and caught up the main Mongol army. No doubt maneuvering out of sight along the ridges of the hills and mountains, Subotai had taken up positions on either side of the axis of advance that the Chin armies were expected to take as they descended upon the plain. There they had waited until the Mongol and Chin armies were fully engaged before taking the Chin armies by surprise on their flanks. Attacked from four directions, the huge Chin army was annihilated at the battle of Shansi. The entire province lay open before the Mongols. Map 3.3 portrays the initial phase of the Mongol-Chin War leading up to and following the battle of Shansi.

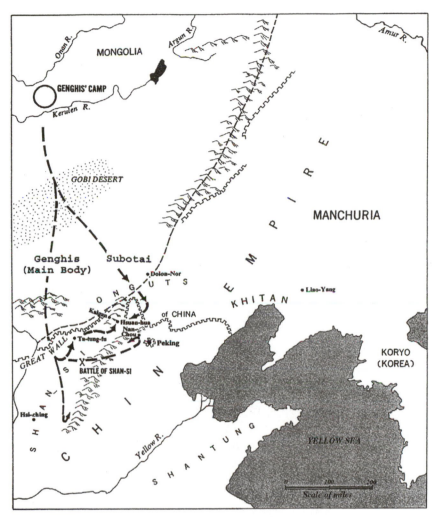

Map 3.3 The War against the Chin: Initial Phase, 1211–1215

KOREA

After the victory at Shansi, the Mongols spent three years marching up and down the land of the Chin, burning, butchering, and defeating one army after another. Still, the Chin emperor refused to surrender, and the mighty citadel of Peking refused to capitulate to the attackers. Here and there Chin generals defected to the Mongols, and at one point forty-six divisions of

Chin troops were in service to the Mongols.[7] Some of these larger units must have had siege units attached to them, and it is a reasonable assumption that it may have been during this period that the Mongols first became acquainted with sophisticated Chinese siege machinery and its manner of operation. This lesson would be put to good use in later engagements against the Muslims and the West. Genghis divided his army into three task forces and set them loose across the Chin landscape. One of these, commanded by Kasar, Genghis' brother, moved east toward southern Manchuria, a second under Juji, Genghis' son, moved south across the plateau of Shansi province, and a third under the khan himself marched southeast through the low Chinese plain. Within six months these task forces sacked and burned ninety towns and forts, and the countryside was laid waste. Corpses rotted in the fields while others floated down the rivers.[8]

Despite the terrible destruction, the Chin refused to surrender and the emperor remained safe behind the walls of the capital. The Mongols had never encountered a country the size of China and were bewildered at the ability of the Chin to resist. Gradually, Genghis began to understand that an army the size of his could never truly conquer and occupy a land of China's vastness. Still, much damage had been done and the Chin armies had been severely weakened. It would be years, or so Genghis believed, before the Chin could recover and threaten Mongolia again. So it was that Genghis Khan opened peace negotiations with the Chin that led to an unsteady peace. For his part, Genghis was content to withdraw his booty-burdened armies back beyond the Great Wall. It was too late in the season to brave the heat of a summer crossing of the Gobi, and the great khan retired to Dolon-nor to wait out the summer. His army was burdened with thousands of Chin prisoners, both military and civilian, who would have to be fed. They were of no further use to him, and Genghis Khan ordered their extermination on the spot.

Less than a year after the peace with the Mongols, the Chin emperor moved his capital from Peking to Kai-feng-fu (modern Nanking) on the far side of the Yellow River. Peking had become too vulnerable to Mongol attack, whereas Kai-feng-fu was more defensible and further away from the Mongol armies. Genghis saw the move as an indication that the Chin emperor did not intend to live up to his word and was planning to resume hostilities. Within months the Chin general Wan-yen began raising new armies and rebuilding the old fortifications. As if rising suddenly out of the ground, these armies marched north against the Khitans. The independence of the Khitan prince and his country was guaranteed by the treaty between the Chin and the Mongols, so when the Chin's military attacked, the Khitans called on Genghis to honor his obligation to them. Never one to leave an ally in the lurch, Genghis sent an army under Mukhali to the Khitan's defense. Ever willing to seek opportunities in others' misfortunes, Genghis also sent a second army under Subotai to punish Manchuria, the original homeland of the Chin. In the fall and early winter of 1214, Subotai descended upon Manchuria like a whirlwind, bringing death and destruction in his wake, a punishment to those who displeased the great khan.

Then a strange thing happened. His original mission accomplished, Subotai turned his columns south and crossed the Yalu River, the border between Korea and Manchuria. Just why Subotai undertook such an attack is unclear, but it is surmised by some scholars that Subotai was in pursuit of Chin units that were retreating before him, and that he therefore had no intention of conquering Korea.[9] Subotai's army probably did not exceed two or three toumans and was, in any case, not sufficient to fight a sustained campaign on the Korean peninsula. His advance units encountered only limited resistance, however, and Subotai pressed southward until he arrived at the outskirts of the capital of Pyongyang. The Korean army was a significant force and the countryside was dotted with fortresses and strong points that could have hindered Subotai's advance. Instead, the Koreans submitted peacefully and the army remained in its garrisons.

Henthorn suggests that the reasons for the Korean accommodation were geopolitical and quite sound. Korea had always survived as an independent kingdom by establishing a tributary relationship with whoever was the dominant power in Manchuria. Whether it was the Khitans, the Chin, or the Jurchids before them, the Koreans survived by recognizing their superiority and accommodating their needs accordingly. The Korean acquiescence in the Mongol incursion was premised upon their perception that the Mongols were now the dominant power in Manchuria to which Korea had to submit, and so it did. As events turned out, the Mongols were not sufficiently powerful to maintain their control of Manchuria and when that became apparent, the Koreans severed their relationship with the Mongols by open warfare.[10] This led to a period of sporadic warfare that lasted almost thirty years. In 1218, the Mongols launched a major invasion of Korea, and, in 1231, Genghis' successor, Ogedai, launched another attack as part of a larger campaign to bring the Chin to their knees once and for all. These events led to the eventual incorporation of Korea into the Mongol empire as a tribute state obligated to the great khan.

THE ATTACK ON KAI-FENG-FU

Peking finally fell to the Mongols in 1215. Genghis remained at Dolon-nor for another two years. Events in Mongolia and on the western frontier required his attention, and in 1217 Genghis Khan returned to Mongolia never again to set foot on Chinese soil. Mukhali was left behind with two toumans of Mongols and several Khitan divisions to continue operations against the Chin. Mukhali campaigned in China for seven years (1217–1223) and succeeded in confining the Chin armies to Honan (Hunan) province. In 1217, he captured the mighty fortress of Tamin, the citadel of central Hopei province, and a year later occupied the capital and several major fortresses of Shansi province. Despite one brilliant campaign after another, Mukhali, like Genghis before him, could not bring about a strategic decision. China was still an enormous landmass bristling with natural defenses and man-made fortifications and populated by 50,000,000 people, and no amount of Mongol military brilliance in the field could change these circumstances. The Mongols found themselves trapped in a long war of attrition, which they could not hope to win with a handful of toumans. Nonetheless, Mukhali pressed on until his death in 1223. He was replaced by another commander, and the war dragged on, borne now mostly by Khitan and Jurchid auxiliaries under Mongol command. In one area, however, the Mongol experience in China proved valuable, and that was in learning how to conduct siege warfare. Using captured Chinese engineers, the Mongols learned how to employ the sophisticated Chinese siege engines and to coordinate the various elements of a siege in a concerted effort to destroy the Chin fortifications. When the Mongol armies returned home, these siege engines and their Chinese crews accompanied them and were employed in the later Mongol campaigns against the Muslims and the West.

Genghis Khan died in 1227 and two years later the Mongol *kurultai* elected his son Ogedai to replace him. Although a competent intellect, Ogedai preferred the comfort of the court to the rough life on horseback. Moreover, he was prone to drunkenness. Because he was unable to impose a clear will on Mongol foreign policy, a struggle for the khan's support broke out among his advisors, split between those who thought the empire was large enough and those, led by Subotai, who thought that there was still much to be done. Subotai reminded Ogedai that the Chin emperor was still safe in his new citadel beyond the Yellow River, and that the southern empire of the Sung had not yet been touched. Far to the west were the lands of the Russian princes and the kings of Europe, all awaiting conquest by the Mongols. Subotai was now fifty-four years old, the last of the original *orloks* of Genghis Khan. All the rest—Jebe, Kublai, Bogorchu, Jelme, and Mukhali—were dead. Subotai, as Carpini noted, was a Mongol of the old school. War and adventure had been his life, and he lived now only to engage in it, for that was the life of a true Mongol. He had no interest in governing empires, only in conquering them. Now Subotai the Valiant, the best of the Mongol generals ever to take the field, convinced his khan that the time had come to renew the war against the Chin. Ogedai's agreement was sealed with the khan's gift of a new wife, a royal princess, to Subotai.[11] Although Ogedai preferred the comforts of court, he was still his father's son, and took the field in nominal command of the operation against the Chin. Nevertheless, Subotai planned the campaign, and Subotai carried it out, commanding the armies in the field. Tuli, Ogedai's brother, was also given a field command, but Subotai was careful to insure that the generals in command of Tuli's toumans were experienced field commanders. He did this to make certain that Tuli's units operated according to the overall plan.

The Chin emperor had abandoned Peking and relocated his capital at Kai-feng-fu, in the fertile lands of Honan province. Here he was safe behind formidable natural barriers. Immediately to the north of the city was the swift and broad Yellow River; to the west lay the range of mountains called the Blue Mountains with their fortified passes and strong citadel at Tung-kuan; and to the south the Yangtze River guarded the capital's rear. Far to the rear was the ocean. The Chin armies would fight well, for there was little strategic depth to trade for time and no way to avoid death if they failed on the field of battle. The Honan plain was dotted with strong points and citadels to slow any advance against the capital; the capital itself was surrounded by 40 miles of fortified walls and contained four million souls.[12] The Chin Empire was still rich and powerful. Moreover, they maintained large armies. But the experience of the Chin generals with the Mongols had taught them a valuable lesson, that their armies were terribly vulnerable to Mongol tactics and ferocity when deployed on open ground. The Chin generals did not intend to meet the Mongols in open battle. Instead, they went over to the defensive, positioning their armies among the forward fortifications and strong points, inviting the Mongols to waste themselves against them.

Subotai, too, had learned from his experiences in earlier campaigns against the Chin. He understood the futility of throwing his armies against the walled citadels, deep rivers, and flooded plains. Even for a Mongol, the

Chinese terrain was a challenge. If he was to defeat the Chin, some way had to be found to draw their armies out of their defenses and engage them on open ground. To be sure, the initial stages of the campaign would require that the Mongols attack and subdue the Chin frontier fortresses, but as long as these objectives were of marginal size, the Mongol siege corps could defeat them without large losses to the Mongol armies. But the Chin could not be defeated one fortress at a time. The attacks on the frontier fortresses were of value only insofar as they convinced the Chinese that the main attack was coming from the north while another Mongol army came at them from an entirely different direction. Then, perhaps, the Chin generals could be forced to take the field. If they did, then the Mongol armies could rapidly concentrate their forces and annihilate them.

The key to Subotai's plan was to keep the Chin armies facing north and west. The Mongols staged from Peking and the Chin naturally assumed that an attack from the north was the most logical direction of advance. The Chin defenses were strongest to the north and west, and when Subotai moved the left wing of the Mongol army (along with its siege machinery) and began to bring the northern defenses along the Yellow River under attack, the Chin generals moved their main forces to resist the crossing of the river. Subotai first reduced the frontier forts and then brought several separate river fortresses under attack in preparation for crossing the river itself. This method of attack, more Chinese than Mongol in nature, took a long time to produce results. Nevertheless, it was time well spent, for while the Chin generals were occupied with Subotai's attack in the north, far to the west the instrument of their eventual destruction was already on the march.

Subotai had sent three toumans (30,000 men), under the nominal command of Tuli but operationally commanded by experienced generals, on a wide sweep to the west and south. Tuli's army was to cross the most barren end of the Gobi, turning south and passing through the Great Wall into the mountain ranges of western China, from which Tuli's men could see the mountain peaks of Tibet in the distance. Climbing through the trails of Szechuan province, Tuli's men were to descend into the fertile valleys of the Sung. Subotai reasoned that the Sung, always eager to weaken their Chin enemies, would do little to stop the Mongol advance and, indeed, they stood aside as Tuli's columns passed through their territory. Once in open terrain, Tuli quickly crossed the upper Wei River and turned north into the mountains between the plain and the capital itself. Passing through the mountains, he gained the flatlands below and marched in the direction of Kai-feng-fu.

Once more, bad news arrived in the Chinese capital, this time from the south. Tuli's army had moved completely undetected and achieved strategic surprise. The intelligence reports that finally reached the Chin generals must have exaggerated the size of Tuli's force, for they concluded that Subotai's army attacking across the Yellow River had been only a feint and that the main Mongol armies were approaching from the south. To meet the threat, the Chin generals ordered the main armies guarding the northern defenses to withdraw from their fortifications and march rapidly back toward the capital to deploy between it and the Mongol armies approaching from the south. With the river garrisons weakened, Subotai prepared a major attack to cross the river and march on the Chin capital.

Although already in position to attack the capital, Tuli waited while the Chin armies redeployed to meet his advance. Before undertaking his great ride to the west, Tuli had asked the more experienced Subotai what it would be like to fight against the Chin. Subotai told him, "They are town-bred people, and so they cannot endure fatigue. Harry them enough and you will find it easy to overcome them in battle."[13] Tuli took the lesson to heart, and began to harass the Chin armies now appearing in front of him. The long ride and difficult conditions of Tuli's march had thinned his armies. It was now autumn and the cold of the mountains through which he had passed, and which now stood behind him, was severe. Tuli decided to test the wisdom of Subotai's advice. He undertook a series of small raids against the Chin positions, hoping to draw their units after him. The Chin generals, seeing the weakened condition of the Mongol columns, ordered a large-scale attack. Tuli retreated slowly up into the mountains to his rear, fighting rearguard and harassing actions as he went. The Mongol ability to maneuver over difficult terrain was considerably better than that of the Chin infantry that pursued them, and on several occasions, Tuli's units were able to circle behind the Chin and destroy their baggage trains. Mongol archers also took a high toll on the Chin infantry as they scrambled over the difficult ground. As the Chinese pressed onward, Tuli retreated higher and higher into the cold and snow of the mountains. It was now winter and the snowstorms began; the cold caused great loss of life among the Chin troops. The Mongols were used to the cold, and much better equipped with their capes and hats to ward off the weather. Still, circumstances were difficult, as the Mongol supplies were exhausted and the game grew scarce. The Mongols ate the flesh of their horses and, in some instances, even the flesh of the dead. Yet as difficult as conditions were, they afflicted the ranks of the Chin even more. The Chin

Map 3.4   Subotai's Attack on Kai-feng-fu

generals had been too quick to pursue the Mongol columns, and now the weather was destroying their armies with each passing day. Still, it might all be worth it if they could trap and destroy the main Mongol army in the mountains. The problem was, however, that Tuli's army was not the Mongol main force.

While the Chin armies were chasing Tuli, Subotai and the main force overcame the frontier garrisons and crossed the Yellow River. The Chin garrisons on the south bank had been weakened when their main units were shifted south to meet Tuli's advance, and were quickly overwhelmed by Subotai's attacks. Having believed Tuli's columns to be the main Mongol army, the Chin generals had fallen for Tuli's feint and were now badly positioned to meet Subotai's advance from the north. In near panic, they ordered their troops to break contact with Tuli, turn around, and march north to intercept Subotai's armies. Seeing the Chin army retreating before him, Tuli stopped his own retreat and went over to the offensive, incessantly attacking and harassing the Chin rear as they attempted to reposition themselves to meet Subotai's advance. So furious and frequent were Tuli's attacks, that, by the time the Chin armies could see the capital in the distance, they were greatly disorganized from their hasty retreat.

Subotai had lured the Chin army from its defensive positions by sheer brilliance of maneuver. First, he had convinced them that there would be a single attack from the north while Tuli maneuvered far to the west, eventually threatening Kai-feng-fu from the south. Convinced that Tuli's army was the main force, the Chin had weakened their positions on the Yellow River to meet the challenge to their west. This permitted Subotai to cross the river and advance on the capital while the Chin armies were busy trying to deal with Tuli. Too late, they realized that Tuli's maneuver had been a feint and that Subotai's main force was bearing down upon them from the north. The Chin needed time to delay Subotai's columns so that the armies in the south could be redeployed to meet his attack. The Chin generals ordered the dikes on the rivers around the capital to be destroyed in an effort to flood the ground, but many years of fighting the Chin had led Subotai to anticipate this tactic. He had already sent units far to his front with the mission to seize the dikes and hold them against any Chin attack. By the time the Chin armies from the south had arrived within sight of the capital, Tuli was hot on their heels.

Subotai's army had closed the distance between himself and the enemy armies to position himself between the Chin armies and the capital. By sheer brilliance of maneuver, Subotai had trapped both the northern and southern Chin armies in open country and cut off their retreat. They had been penned in like a herd of cattle, and the Mongol columns, using speed, maneuver, and firepower, butchered the Chin without mercy. Inside the city walls, the emperor and one million inhabitants were trapped. Within days, Subotai brought the city under siege. Pleased at the victories of his generals, Ogedai, along with Tuli, left China for the steppe, leaving Subotai in command with instructions to destroy the city.

At the beginning of the Chin wars, the Mongols' ability to successfully overwhelm cities was primitive and usually failed. Now, after almost twenty years of war, the Mongols had mastered the secrets of siegecraft. Subotai now brought the full panoply of Chinese siege equipment and manpower to bear against the Chin capital. First, he trapped the defenders inside and removed any hope of escape by constructing a wooden wall of contravallation that extended for fifty-four miles![14] Mongol catapults with Chinese crews kept up a continual barrage of firepots to set the city's buildings afire. Local captives were forced to pile brush against the walls and set the wood ablaze. Thousands fell in this effort as the Chin defenders showed no hesitation to fire upon their own people. The Chin defenders responded with catapult and mangonels of their own and even employed the dreaded *ho pao*. If we may trust the somewhat vague descriptions of this weapon, the ho pao seems to have been a long bamboo tube thrust out from holes in the defensive wall, its end coming to rest near Mongol positions or machines. Probably ignited by a timed slow-burning fuse, these bamboo tubes exploded, leaving a black and smoking crater in the earth. It is unlikely that the idea of using shot in this sort of primitive cannon dawned on the Chinese, but there was no doubt that the ho pao was a powerful psychological weapon even as its killing effects on personnel were probably not impressive.

For six days, Subotai's army assaulted the city with scaling ladders, but to no avail. It was during this time that the Chinese records tell of an intriguing incident. A Chin officer, perhaps a general, who had been captured by the Mongols and brought into the camp asked his captor to point out the great Subotai. Passing by, Subotai overheard the request and spoke to the man. "You who have but a moment to live," Subotai said, "What do you want of me?" The Chin officer replied, "It is not chance but destiny that makes conquerors such as you," he said. "Having seen you, I am ready to die!" The Chinese chroniclers do not record what Subotai's response was, only that the Chin officer was executed as planned.[15]

It was summer, and the heat strangled both attacker and defender alike. Inside the city, starvation was taking a terrible toll. The Chinese chroniclers report that the inhabitants ate what horseflesh they could find, and made soup of saddle leather and bones mixed with green weeds. Even the leather skins from the military drums were eaten. Soon, the Chinese began to kill their prisoners in order to eat their flesh. Then a terrible plague broke out. The speed and maneuver of the Mongol armies usually meant that they did not linger long in one spot so that they mostly remained free of diseases that often crippled other, less mobile armies. Subotai, the old campaigner, recognized the threat the plague outbreak presented to his army if he remained near the city. He opened negotiations with the Chin and offered to lift the siege of the city. As proof of his sincerity, Subotai offered to withdraw his army just beyond sight of the city in return for gifts for his officers. The Chin, perhaps thinking that the siege was over, complied and Subotai withdrew his army away from the locus of infection. While the plagued raged and weakened the defenders, Subotai's army remained unaffected. He was joined by a division of Chinese troops provided by the ever-opportunistic Sung. Within a month, Subotai ordered his army to attack the city once more. This time the Mongols breached the walls and a great slaughter began. The Chin emperor committed suicide in despair as the city's collapse took with it the last vestige of Chin power.

Ever the old Mongol, Subotai wanted to turn the city over to his men to loot and kill as they wished, for this was the Mongol custom and the resistance of the city had angered Subotai. Moreover, Subotai saw no value at all in the towns and plowed fields of the Chinese plain. Better, he advised, to kill all who lived there and turn the plain into fine horse breeding country. Who cared for farms and towns when it was the Mongols' life to ride, roam, and fight? But Ogedai Khan had come to trust the wisdom of his Chinese advisors, who pointed out that there was more loot to be had in the form of future taxes if the city and their craftsmen were left to their trades and the farmers to their fields. Thus, Ogedai overruled Subotai, sparing the Chin capital and the people of China from a terrible fate. Leaving Mongol detachments behind to keep the peace, Subotai returned to the steppe, to Karakorum, the new capital that Ogedai had begun building two years before. He then turned his attention to fulfilling the dream he had carried with him for more than a decade, the conquest of Russia and the West.

4 HURRICANE FROM THE EAST

In 1217, Genghis Khan and the Mongol army returned to Mongolia, leaving Mukhali behind to prosecute the war against the Chin. Subotai, who had planned or influenced many of the campaigns fought by the Mongols until now, seems to have become the equivalent of the Mongol chief-of-staff. From this period forward we find him always located with Genghis and the main force when campaigning, rather than holding a field command. Only after the campaigns were well underway, or when Genghis required a trusted general to undertake some important operational mission, did Subotai take the field as a troop commander. The Mongol habit of placing the khan's sons in nominal command of field armies often obscures the role of Subotai and other commanders in the actual operations, even though it is quite certain that it was the trusted generals (and not the khan's sons) who actually planned and executed military operations. After Genghis Khan's death in 1227, his successor, Ogedai, seems to have left all the planning and execution of military operations to Subotai, who then assumed a more formalized position as chief of staff of the Mongol armies, one that he had already held in practice while Genghis was still alive. Thus, the wars against Kara Khitai and the Khwarizmian Shah were planned by Subotai.

Once back in Mongolia, Genghis decided to settle old scores with the Naiman and Merkits, against whom he had fought a decade ago, driving them to the western borders of Mongolia. Genghis had killed the Merkit chief, Toqto'a Beki, in 1208, during the tribal wars, but his son and the remnants of the tribe had fled and settled somewhere northwest of Lake Balkhash.[1] As a military force the Merkits presented no threat to the Mongols and, aside from personal vengeance, Genghis' motives in attacking them remain unclear. Whatever his motives were, they must have been of some import, for he assigned Subotai to command the operation against the Merkits. While the strength of Subotai's army is not known, it has been reasonably calculated to be two *toumans* (or 20,000 men).

Of far greater strategic significance for the security of Mongolia's borders was the situation with the Naimans and their renegade chief, Kuchlug. Along with the remnants of his tribe, Kuchlug had fled from Mongolia to Kara Khitai after his father was defeated and killed by Genghis during the tribal wars. Kara Khitai lay to the west-southwest of Mongolia proper and included what is now the northeastern part of modern Turkestan, a portion of Chinese Turkestan, and the area around Lake Balkhash. Although the governors of Kara Khitai were originally Chinese, most of the population was Turkic. After the defeat of his father, Kuchlug and his tribe fled to Kara Khitai were they were welcomed by its king, Yeluu Zhilugu, who soon offered Kuchlug his daughter in marriage and made him a high official. Kuchlug reorganized his tribal remnants into a powerful military force, and, in 1211, undertook a coup d état against the old king and took power as ruler of the country. Kuchlug was a Naiman of the Nestorian faith and a Mongol, factors that made the mostly Turkic-Muslim population suspicious of him from the beginning. Eager to insure the control of his realm, Kuchlug formed an alliance with the Muslim Khwarizmian Shah who, for his own reasons of state (and an ambition to eventually absorb Kara Khitai into his realm), supported Kuchlug in his wars against his own people. Kuchlug pursued a policy of forced conversion of the Muslim populace that resulted in a reign of religious terror against the population, even with the support of the Muslim Shah. By the time Genghis planned to move against him, Kuchlug had lost the support of his own people. Even his alliance with the Shah was disrupted, leading the Shah to undertake sporadic border raids against the country along the Syr Darya River, which formed the border of the two realms.

Two Mongol armies converged on Kara Khitai, each with its own objectives but operating in concert and in support of one another. Jebe, in command of two toumans, composed the main force targeted against Kara Khitai itself; its mission was to conquer the country and kill or capture Kuchlug. The second army, also of 20,000 men, was commanded by Subotai. Its primary mission was to attack and destroy the Merkits living in an area along the route of advance. Following this, Subotai's army was to march ahead and to the south of Jebe's column to protect its flank as Jebe's force moved in trail into Kara Khitai proper. Here we see Subotai's brilliant strate-

gic mind at work. The Mongol intelligence service was well aware of events
in Kara Khitai, especially the broken alliance with the Shah and his territorial
ambitions in Kara Khitai. A Mongol defeat of Kuchlug risked creating a vac-
uum in the country that the Shah might be tempted to fill by undertaking
military operations of his own, perhaps crossing the Syr Darya River and
occupying substantial parts of the country. It was standard Mongol tactical
practice to never permit an enemy force to occupy a threatening position,
relative to a flank of the Mongol's main body. In this case, Subotai raised the
tactical practice to a strategic level. His army would precede Jebe's main
force, protecting his flank from any attack by the Shah. To this end, Subotai
marched his army quickly through Merkit territory, sweeping aside the Merkits as he went and heading straight for the border between Kara-Khitai and
Khwarizm, positioning himself to intercept any movements by the Shah.
The maneuver was to have great consequences for the future.

The two Mongol armies moved in tandem along, and eventually across,
the Altai and Tarbagatai mountains to Almaliq. Once through the mountains, Jebe moved south of Lake Balkhash directly into Kara Khitai. Subotai
moved more southwest toward the border.[2] In an excellent example of the
proposition that wars are always fought within a political context, Jebe proceeded through Kara Khitai with a minimum of violence. He proclaimed
that all Muslims were to have complete religious freedom and that none of
their holy places would be harmed. In each town he came to the mosques
were reopened and no plundering or atrocities were carried out by the army.
One city after another threw open its gates to the Mongols until Kuchlug
was forced to flee from his capital and seek refuge in the mountains. The
Mongols pursued the Naiman prince and "chased him like a mad dog" until
he was trapped in the Sarykol valley, high in the Pamir Mountains, and taken
by a group of local hunters who promptly turned him over to the Mongols.
Jebe had Kuchlug beheaded on the spot. In honor of his victory, Jebe sent
Genghis a gift of 1,000 chestnut horses with white muzzles for which Kara
Khitai was famous.

While Jebe conducted operations in the north, to the southwest Subotai
prowled the border for any sign of Mohammed Shah. The Shah was aware of
the Mongols and the reputation of their great chief, Genghis Khan. After the
fall of Peking to the Mongols, the Shah had sent an embassy to the khan's
court to propose the establishment of trade relations and to find out all he
could about the power and habits of the Mongols. Genghis had welcomed
the overture, and had already dispatched a return envoy to Mohammed. The

Shah knew of the fierce reputation of the Mongol armies and, if we can trust the Muslim chroniclers, wished to see for himself how fierce the Mongol soldiers were. The Shah himself had recently undertaken a raid into Kara Khitai, and, once made aware of Subotai's presence, ordered his army to attack Subotai. Unfortunately, the chroniclers did not preserve an account of the battle, except to say that it was fiercely fought on both sides until darkness put an end to it. During the night Subotai broke contact and withdrew, leaving the Shah with little more than the battlefield dead to contemplate in the morning light. Although the skirmish was inconclusive in a tactical sense, the Muslim chroniclers tell us that Mohammed Shah was deeply impressed by the valor and maneuverability of Subotai's troops, so much so that he began to have serious doubts about the ability of his own mercenary troops to deal with them in open battle. It is an old maxim (attributed to Napoleon) that a commander ought never to take counsel of his fears. In the case of Mohammed Shah, it was sound advice; however, unfortunately for him, it was advice that he rejected. He had seen the enemy's teeth. Now Mohammed Shah, whose people called him the Second Alexander, was frightened to his bones.[3]

THE WAR AGAINST THE SHAH

With Jebe's successful conquest of Kara Khitai there was no longer a geographic buffer between the empire of the Mongols and that of the Khwarizmian Shah. Any miscalculation by either side would bring both empires into collision, with dire consequences. After the fall of Peking, the Shah had sent an ambassador to Genghis' court proposing the establishment of relations between the two empires. Even as events unfolded in Kara Khitai, Genghis had dispatched an ambassador to the court of the Shah bearing a large gold nugget from China as a gift. In 1218, the two sides reached an agreement concerning trade, and Genghis dispatched a caravan from Mongolia consisting of 450 men (mostly Muslims) and 500 camels laden with expensive goods to the Shah. More important was a man named Uqana, who carried a personal message from Genghis to the Shah. The caravan and its Mongol ambassador crossed the border and stopped at Otrar.

The governor of Otrar, a relative of the Shah, suspected the caravan of being full of spies and arrested its members, including Genghis' ambassador, Uqana. The Muslim governor wanted to execute the merchants and seize their goods. When he made this request to the Shah, the Shah agreed and the merchants were killed. One of the camel drivers escaped the slaughter and made his way back to Mongolia where he informed the khan of what happened. Although furious, Genghis remained ever the pragmatic leader. Instead of seeking vengeance, Genghis sent another embassy to the Shah; this one comprised a Muslim and two Mongols. Perhaps, Genghis may have thought, the Shah's governor had simply exceeded his authority and, if so, the matter could be put to rest by the governor's execution. When the Mongol ambassadors made this request of the Shah, it was refused. Worse, the Shah ordered the Muslim killed and the beards of the Mongols shaved off. The Mongols returned to Mongolia with the tale of the new outrage. This time there would be no reprieve. Genghis Khan declared war against Mohammed Shah, sovereign of the empire of Khwarizm, and mobilized his army.

The incident at Otrar turned out to be one of the most momentous accidents of history. The actions of an obscure government official set in motion a chain of events that changed the world. Until this incident, there was no evidence that Genghis Khan was dissatisfied with the borders of the great empire he had established for the Mongols. Now, the events at Otrar forced him to move against the Shah, with the result that all of Persia eventually came under Mongol rule. This, in turn, led to Subotai's reconnaissance into the Russian steppes, which provided the intelligence for the Mongol attack and occupation of Russia, an occupation that lasted for three centuries! And the success of the Russian campaign led inevitably to Subotai's assault against Eastern Europe. No one foresaw it at the time, but the murder of the Mongol caravan at Otrar changed the entire history of Central Asia, Russia, and the West.

The original state of Khwarizm was located between the two great rivers, the Amu Darya, the Oxus of the ancients, and the Syr Darya, known to the ancients as the Jaxartes. Both rivers emptied into the salty Aral Sea, six hundred miles distant. The northern portion of the country was composed of half fertile river valley land and half desert, crisscrossed by caravan roads that connected a series of walled cities and fortresses. The kingdom's two greatest cities, Bokhara, the city of scholars, and Samarkand, the capital, sat at the center of these trade routes, as well as at the center of the strategic equation. The original fief had been given to Ala ad-Din, the father of Mohammed II, by the Sultan of the Seljuks, who appointed him viceroy over the area. During incessant wars, Mohammed II, now Shah of Khwarizm, had expanded his father's holdings in almost every direction. He subdued the lands to the north across the Syr Darya all the way to the Kirgiz Steppe and conquered

Transoxiana along with the cities of Samarkand, which he made his capital, and Fergana. In the south, he invaded Afghanistan and subdued its wild tribes. His military conquests were so extensive that he was called the Second Alexander and the Shadow of Allah upon Earth. The armies of the Shah were formidable, and chroniclers suggest that they numbered 400,000 troops.[4] The empire's manpower base was enormous and capable of providing thousands of troops in a national emergency.

Any Mongol attack on Khwarizm was complicated by a number of factors beyond the size and combat power of the Shah's armies. The distance involved was enormous. From the upper waters of the Irtysh River (in the land of the Uighurs) where Genghis assembled his army to the Syr Darya (Khwarizm's northern border) was almost 1,300 miles. The first strategic target beyond the river, the oasis of Zarafshan, where the capital of Samarkand lay, in the province of Bokhara was almost 300 miles farther.[5] The terrain over which the Mongol army had to move was some of the most difficult in the world. Unlike China, where the Mongols could gain entry to the country at any point along a 300-mile border, the empire of the Shah was protected by ranges of nearly impassable mountains, some over 20,000 feet high, steep valleys, and gorges where snow lingered even until summer. Genghis' decision to make the march from late autumn to spring exposed the Mongol army to terrible hardships from snow, cold, and starvation. Much of the march would have to be made across an almost waterless and foodless desert waste forcing the Mongols to rely more heavily than usual upon carrying their own supplies. Moreover, there was no chance of achieving strategic surprise, for the nature of the terrain over which the army had to travel left it only one axis of advance, down and through the Zungarian Gate, the Gate of Winds, the main pass through which nomad tribes from the Central Asiatic plateau had traveled for ages to reach the West. Unlike the attack on China, the Mongol armies approaching Khwarizm would be detected in sufficient time for the Shah to react. Once over the Syr Darya River, the Mongols would have to face a Muslim army more than twice its size, fighting along internal lines of communication, and supported by scores of walled cities and fortifications. The invasion of the empire of the Shah was a breathtaking undertaking sufficient to give even as brilliant a strategist as Subotai and as great a field general as Genghis Khan pause.

But the great khan was not to be deterred by these difficulties. In the summer of 1218, he began assembling a great army on the banks of the Irtysh River. The war that lay ahead was the first war waged by the Mongols against a Muslim state, and turned into a war of extermination in which four-fifths of the population of the Shah's empire was killed or reduced to slavery.[6] As one historian put it, "more lives were lost, probably, than in any similar conflict of such duration, a mere three years. . . . The cold and deliberate genocide practiced by the Mongols . . . has no parallel save that of the ancient Assyrians and modern Nazis."[7] The Mongol army that assembled for the invasion represented a maximum national effort and required all Mongols between the ages of seventeen and sixty to take up arms. The Mongol vassal states were also required to provide troop contingents. All except Hsi-Hsia met their obligations, a fact which led Genghis to punish that country later. The size of the Mongol army that set out from Irtysh remains a matter of debate. The Russian Orientalist Barthold's estimate of more than 200,000 men seems high. The Mongol army was still recovering from its losses in China, and substantial troop contingents under Mukhali were still operating there. The refusal of Hsi-Hsia to join the campaign would have required that substantial troops be left behind in Mongolia to insure that there was no hostile action from that quarter. Prawdin's suggestion that only 150,000 Mongol troops might have taken part in the war seems somewhat more reasonable,[8] while De Hartog's estimate of 90,000 seems low.[9] Along with the troops would have come 400,000 or so horses, thousands of camels, hundreds of cattle, wagons, etc., in a larger than usual logistics train dictated by the nature of the terrain and expected rigors of the march. To move all of this almost 2,000 miles over some of the most daunting terrain and weather on the globe and still arrive in condition to undertake offensive combat operations was an achievement that might well seem impossible to modern military commanders. Along one section of the march, the segment between Sairam Nor and Almaliq, the Taoist chronicler, Ch'ag Ch'un, says that Jagatai, the second son of the khan, organized the building of the roads and bridges along which the main army passed. "He broke down the rocks of the slopes and built no less than 48 bridges of wood wide enough for two carts to pass over, side by side."[10]

To undertake an invasion of a country so far from one's home base against an enemy whose armies were far more numerous and at least as combat-seasoned as one's own might seem an act of foolhardiness. But military capabilities must always be assessed within the political or social context within which they are employed. Here the Mongol intelligence service had provided Mongol military commanders with important information that suggested that the armies of the Shah might not be as powerful as they appeared to be. First, the empire itself was a recent creation; less than four years had passed since it had been forged in the military conquests of the Shah, and it was full of cracks. The administrative structure was loose and flimsy. Most of the former governmental officials in the provinces that had been removed during the wars had not yet been replaced. Second, the Turkic ruling class was hated by the Persian subject population, and the regime's main support was its army of Turkish mercenaries whose loyalty was always in doubt. Third, the population was oppressed by heavy taxation, and the frequent conflicts between the Shah and the Muslim caliphs alienated the devout that came to see the Shah as an infidel who persecuted his own faith.

In addition, the Shah's army suffered from two major shortcomings. First, many of its troops were from mutually hostile tribal contingents that could not be employed far from their home territory and who often would not fight alongside their tribal enemies. Second, rebellions throughout the empire were frequent, and military garrisons throughout the empire had to be kept at strength to keep the peace and could not, except at grave risk to governmental control, be deployed elsewhere. The Shah's army may have been a huge military juggernaut, but it could not be easily deployed to meet a mobile threat. Again, as the old Mongol proverb had it, "an army of donkeys led by a lion is better than an army of lions led by a donkey." The soaring ambition of the Shah was simply not matched by his grasp of strategy or tactics. The Shah's single experience with Mongol troops had been the clash with Subotai's column a year earlier, and the Shah had come away from that experience convinced that his army was no match for the Mongols in open terrain. Taking counsel of his fears, Mohammed II, the Second Alexander, was about to make a devastating strategic error that would cost him his crown and his life.

Subotai did not rely solely upon intelligence reports gathered by Mongol officers from Muslim merchants and spies. Subotai's campaign planning incorporated two additional elements that served to offset the combat power of the Shah's armies. Khwarizm was a land of walled cities and fortresses that would have to be taken quickly if the Mongol attack was to succeed. The Mongol experience in China had led them to an appreciation of the art of siegecraft in military operations. Under Ogedai's direction, they had begun to assemble a siege train. Now, as the army prepared to move against Khwarizm, the Mongol army was accompanied by a siege train that comprised heavy artillery of the type that the Mongols had first encountered in China. Catapults and mangonels were dismantled and transported on yaks and camels, and here we see the first truly extensive use of camels in the logistics train. The Chinese-manufactured artillery engines were accompanied by Chinese artillerists, along with Chinese engineers who were experts in earthworks and bridge building. If the Shah expected the Mongol attack to falter before the walls of Khwarizm's cities and fortress as it had faltered before the walls of China's cities, the new Mongol artillery and siege units were prepared to prove otherwise.

One of the central difficulties facing Mongol planners was the simple reality that the only approach to Khwarizm passed through the Zungarian Gate, thus depriving the Mongols of the element of strategic surprise while hemming in the scope of maneuver of their advancing columns. The terrain deprived the Mongols of that wide sweep of maneuver and the ability to feint that played such a large part in their strategic thinking. But Subotai had another surprise for the Shah. During Subotai and Jebe's forays into Kara Khitai earlier in the year, Jebe had stumbled upon what appeared to be another route through the mountains leading to the west. To be sure, the terrain and eventual terminus of the alternate route were unknown, but at least the direction was correct. Jebe, with perhaps 10,000 men, was sent ahead of the main body of the army to locate the route and prepare to follow it west. The arrow messengers who kept the Mongol columns in contact with the main body reported that Jebe had found the trail. In a bold gamble, Subotai sent reinforcements under the command of Juji, Genghis' son, to Jebe with instructions to press ahead. It was now midwinter.

Jebe's ride across the mountains at the head of an army of 30,000 men into unknown territory makes Hannibal's crossing of the Alps pale in comparison. The Mongol column entered the cleft between the Pamir and Tian Shan mountains in the dead of winter, often riding through snow five and six feet deep. It was so cold that the horses' legs froze and they had to be wrapped in yak hide to prevent them from becoming useless. The Mongol ponies had learned the trick of scraping away the snow with their hooves to get at the grass beneath, and even ate leaves from trees and bushes. The Mongols themselves were wrapped in their *dachas*, their double-sheepskin coats, which protected them against the cold as they crossed the passes of the Kisil-Art and the Terek-Davan, both at a height of 13,000 feet. Along the route the Mongols had abandoned their baggage and heavy equipment to lighten the load on the army. Soon they began to eat the horses. Exhausted, frozen, and malnourished, many Mongol soldiers died in the snow and left behind, frozen in the white world of the Asian mountains.[11] Jebe pressed on despite the losses, and after three months of enduring these terrible conditions, his ragged, half-starved, and weakened army descended into the Fergana Valley. Here spring had already arrived and the grass, vineyards, and wheat fields were in full bloom. Map 4.1, which appears later, shows the route of march of Jebe's army along with the routes of advance of the other Mongol columns.

While Jebe was struggling across the roof of the world, the main Mongol armies had descended through the Gate of the Winds and were moving toward the Syr Darya River, the northern border of Khwarizm. All winter long, the Mongol army had been subjected to terrible cold and hunger as it pressed forward. The fierce *burans*, or black windstorms, created such frigid wind chills that the cattle herds froze to death. The Mongol ponies could find so little to eat that a Chinese chronicler, Ye Liu Chutsai, reported that the animals began to bleed at their veins. All along the way, the soldiers were forced to fell large trees to build bridges across the many gorges and crevasses in their path. Many soldiers died of the cold and exhaustion. In early March, even before the snow melted, the main body made their way out onto the western steppe and rode swiftly around Lake Balkhash. By the time the first grass was pressing up through the earth, they were making their way over the last barrier of the Black Range and moving straight toward the border of the Khwarizmian Empire.

As the main Mongol army pressed on, Jebe's column was far to the front and to the south entering the Fergana Valley. Now fortune smiled on the Mongols. The Shah's intelligence service detected Jebe's column in the Fergana as he foraged for food and horses to replenish his men. The Shah ordered up a large army, perhaps 50,000 men, and personally took command as it moved into the Fergana Valley to deal with the Mongol intruders. Surprised and greatly outnumbered, Jebe wanted to break contact and head back into the mountains, perhaps hoping to draw the Shah's troops after him and into an ambush. But Juji, Genghis' son and the nominal commander of the expedition, thought it cowardly to retreat and ordered the Mongol column into the attack. In a splendid display of Mongol military discipline, Jebe's exhausted and outnumbered troops moved quickly to engage the armies of the Shah.

There are two versions of the battle that followed, both of which are plausible. In one version, the terrain of the valley and the exhaustion of the Mongols and their mounts forced them to forego their usual tactical maneuvers and attack head-on with their heavy cavalry.[12] In this version, the shock of the attack and the bravery of the Mongol troops carried the day. In the other version of the battle, the Mongols displayed their usual tactical brilliance, using their light cavalry to ride across the enemy front in successive waves to weaken the Shah's main force with arrow fire before committing the heavy cavalry. In this version, the Shah himself was almost captured by a Mongol unit that had penetrated the line and made a dashing attempt to strike at the enemy commander. Whatever the case, nightfall brought an end to the fight. Jebe, knowing that he was outnumbered, wisely broke contact in the dark and retreated taking the extra horses, wounded, and looted cattle and supplies with them. At dawn, the Shah was left with only an empty battlefield littered with the dead of both sides.

When reports reached Genghis and Subotai with the main body, Subotai immediately ordered reinforcements sent to Jebe with instructions for the column to divide into two forces. One, of perhaps 10,000 men (probably the smaller of the two), was assigned to Jebe with instructions that he was to press down the Amu Darya across the Hindu Kush Mountains and engage the Shah's armies wherever he could. Having attracted the Shah's attention to the Fergana with Jebe's raid, the longer it could be focused there, the more time and cover the main Mongol columns would have to move closer to the border. The other column of perhaps 20,000 was assigned to Juji, with instructions to follow on through the Fergana Valley protecting the flank of a larger Mongol column, under Jagatai and Ogedai, and to cross the river striking at Khojend. With their exposed flank secured, the main body of the Mongol army broke up into large columns and continued to move toward the border. They had come more than 1,200 miles in less than four months.

The clashes with Subotai's army in Kara Khitai earlier in the year and the battle with Jebe in the Fergana Valley convinced the Shah that his army was no match for the Mongols on open ground. The Shah was also aware of the Mongol experience in China, and now bet heavily that their ability to besiege cities was not much improved. Khwarizm was a kingdom of great cities and fortresses, and the Shah went over to the defensive to make maximum strategic use of these assets. His large army was deployed forward, in the garrisons along the main rivers, to protect the large towns of Bokhara, Samarkand, and Urgench. Unwilling to attempt to preempt the Mongol advance north of the Syr Darya River, he would tempt the Mongols to lay siege to the cities. Strengthened by powerful garrisons, his hope was that the Mongols would be unable to overwhelm the cities and, after a season of raiding and plundering, would return home.

It was a strategic mistake of catastrophic proportions, proof of the old maxim that "in military matters, hope is not a method." The Shah's strategy dispersed his strength in defensive positions which, in itself, would not have been fatal had he not dispersed nearly all his forces, leaving himself with an insufficient concentration of forces on hand to deal with any unexpected Mongol attack from elsewhere. The military power base of the empire would permit raising additional armies, especially to the south. But none were on hand to deal with contingencies that might arise from the set of circumstances in which the Shah might immediately find himself. Having deployed his troops, the Shah waited for the Mongol onslaught to begin.

News quickly reached him that Juji's toumans were making their way down the Fergana, taking one town after another. Their ultimate objective could only be either Tashkent or Khojend, both of which contained substantial garrisons. Although Jebe's column had disappeared after the battle, the Shah was not overly concerned. As far as he knew, the Mongol main body was still to his front and approaching the border cities as expected. When word reached him that a Mongol column was attacking Otrar, there was still no sense of urgency. Everything was going as the Shah had expected. And then everything collapsed. News arrived that the Mongols had crossed the Amu Darya 250 miles to the south and were plundering the countryside. This was Jebe's small column of, perhaps, no more than a single touman. He had crossed the Pamir Mountains and was now on the Shah's flank. The Shah had no notion of the strength of Jebe's army, but if it were a major force, the Shah would be cut off from the southern part of his kingdom, Afghanistan, and Khorassan. All of these were significant resources of military manpower. The Shah could not risk losing them and immediately sent his last reserves to intercept and deal with Jebe's advance.

No sooner had the reserves departed to the south than more bad news arrived. For some weeks, the Shah's intelligence service had been unable to locate the main body of the Mongol army that had been approaching from the north and to the front. Now news had arrived that the Mongol army was marching on Samarkand from the west! After Jebe's clash in the Fergana Valley, Subotai had changed the direction of the main army moving far to the north before turning to the south and west. He had crossed the Syr Darya unobserved, marching across the great Kizil Kum desert, a 400-mile-wide arid landscape regarded as impassable. With the help of Turcoman guides, the main force had arrived behind the Shah's defenses. The Mongols crossed the Amu Darya at a town called Nur with Subotai leading the advance guard,[13] thereby achieving complete surprise.

A glance at Map 4.1 shows a complete encirclement of the Shah's defenses. Genghis, Subotai, and the Mongol main army were advancing on Samarkand from the west. In the east, Jagatai and Ogedai had overcome the defenses of Otrar and were marching on the capital even as Juji had stormed Khojend. To the south Jebe's column was advancing as rapidly as possible toward the main sector of activity, threatening to cut off the Shah's retreat in the process. Subotai and the Mongol army had carried out one of the more memorable envelopment movements in military history. Caught in the Mongol trap, the Shah sent what few forces he had with him to reinforce Samarkand. Accompanied only by his bodyguard, Shah Mohammed II, the "Second Alexander," abandoned the field and fled southwest hoping to raise new armies and fight again another day. (The dotted line on Map 4.1 shows the route of the Shah as he fled to Balkh.)

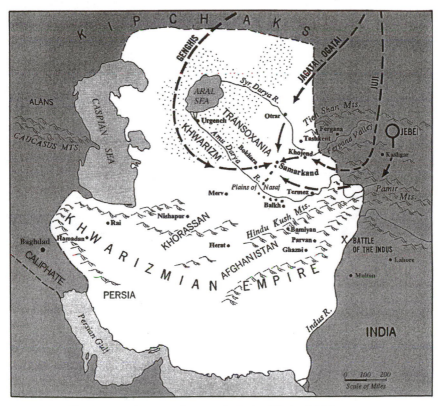

Map 4.1   The Mongol Campaign against the Shah, 1220

The Mongol army moved directly toward the capital of Samarkand, where Subotai thought the Shah was, only to discover that he had fled. With all of the Shah's forces deployed inside the cities of the empire, the Mongols had no fear of an attack from them and could attack the cities at their leisure. It was this sense of security that may have prompted Genghis to order the capture of the Shah, assigning 30,000 men to the task. He sent for Subotai, Jebe, and his son-in-law, Toguchar, placing each one in command of a touman, with Subotai in overall command. The task force was to pursue the Shah and capture him. The Muslim chroniclers report that Genghis told Subotai, "Do not come back until you have taken him prisoner. If he flees before you, follow him through his domains, withersoever he may turn. Spare every town which surrenders to you, but destroy ruthlessly anyone who gets in your way and offers resistance." In addition, Subotai was given a warrant marked with the red seal of the great khan in which he promised that all those who did not resist were to be spared. Anyone who resisted was to be killed. Not only was Subotai to pursue and capture the Shah but also to accept the surrender of all those cities and towns along the way. If necessary, he was to attack and raze those towns that did not submit.

Genghis Khan was a man of his word who kept his promises, even at the cost of his son-in-law, Toguchar. For reasons that remain unclear, Toguchar defied the khan's orders and sacked a town that had surrendered to Jebe. Genghis' first impulse was to have his relative killed. Instead, he sent a common soldier to the general with instructions that Toguchar was to lay down his commission and transfer his troops to Subotai. Then he was to continue to serve in the ranks where, as events turned out, he was killed fighting as a common soldier in an assault on one of the towns.[14]

With Subotai in command, 30,000 Mongol soldiers set out in pursuit of the Shah, crossing the Amu Darya River and following him to Balkh. Except for his bodyguard, the Shah was unattended by troops. At Balkh, he thought of moving toward Afghanistan, but his conquest of that land had been most recent and he did not trust the loyalty of the tribesmen there. Instead, he headed south toward Khorassan and the city of Herat. Even as he fled, the Shah demonstrated some grasp of strategy. Everywhere he went he urged the populace to abandon their fields and homes and to destroy their crops and animals. In the few garrisons he encountered he exhorted them to fight to the last man, to hold the fortresses, until he could return from the west with a new army. The Muslim chroniclers, both Persian and Arab, have charged him with cowardice for these actions, but unfairly so. The Shah was attempting to mount a strategic defense. Like Fabius against Hannibal and Kutuzov in his war against Napoleon, the Shah sought to achieve the same goal: to depopulate the countryside of men and crops in order to deny the Mongol armies food and deprive them of a source of slave labor to use in their assaults against the cities and fortifications. If the cities held out and the countryside deprived the Mongols of food and manpower, the Mongol advance might be delayed long enough for the Shah to raise a new army in the west. Already in the east, his son, Jalal ad-Din, was raising an army.

Map 4.2 shows the route of Subotai's pursuit of Shah Mohammed. Having changed direction again, by the time the Shah reached Merv he had learned of the fall of Samarkand and the attack on Bokhara. Fearful that the Mongols were close, he fled southwest over the mountains to Nishapur. Meanwhile, Subotai had reached Balkh, which surrendered without a fight, where he learned that the Shah had fled to Herat. Eager to close the distance between himself and his quarry, Subotai and his troops rode as much as eighty miles a day, often riding their spare horses to exhaustion. The khan's promise of amnesty for cities that did not resist preceded Subotai so that Herat and Merv opened their gates and provided the Mongols with food and fodder. Between Merv and Nishapur, however, the Mongols encountered resistance from some smaller cities with the result that Damghan, Tus, and Samnan were sacked. The major fortresses were usually bypassed to save time, but in at least one instance, at Savah, they were attacked. It seems that as the Mongol columns passed under the walls, the inhabitants of the city assembled atop the ramparts shouting insults and blowing trumpets at Subotai's troops. Subotai halted his columns and turned on the fortress, taking it in three days. All the inhabitants were killed and the ruins set afire.

For a short time, the Shah stayed at Nishapur. Even within its strong fortifications, he did not feel safe, and so fled further west over mountains and skirting the edge of the desert across the entire region of Persian Iraq. The Mongols reached Nishapur where they overtook the Shah's mother and his harem trying to reach the Shah in Nishapur. The royal treasure was seized and sent back under guard to Samarkand. Outside the city of Rai (modern Tehran), Subotai's columns clashed with a loyal remnant of the Shah's army. Thirty thousand men took the field against the Mongols, but were quickly defeated. Within the city of Rai, the populace was divided into two factions, one that favored resistance and one that favored surrender. The two sides came to blows with the faction favoring the Mongols gaining the upper hand and slaughtering the other faction in the streets. Subotai rode into the city

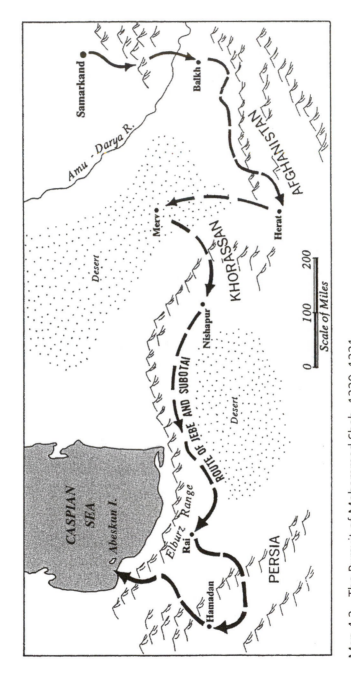

Map 4.2   The Pursuit of Mohammed Shah, 1220–1221

and watched with fascination as the two sides killed one another. At last, the pro-Mongol faction carried the day only to have Subotai turn his troops upon them. Who could trust such men, Subotai must have thought. And then he ordered the extermination of every male in the city.

Between Rai and Hamadan the Mongols almost caught up with the Shah, and may have wounded him in a skirmish near there. Furious at missing their quarry, Subotai ordered an attack on the small settlements of Zanjan and Kazvin. Between Hamadan and the shore of the Caspian Sea, the Mongols lost the trail only to pick it up again and close rapidly on the Shah. Muslim legend has it that Subotai arrived on the shore of the sea only to see a sail in the distance carrying the Shah to safety. His men were so angry at having failed, so the legend goes, that some of them charged their mounts into the sea swimming after him until they drowned. Subotai reported his failure back to Genghis saying only that the Shah had escaped to some distant land north of the Caspian Sea. He could not know, of course, that the Shah reached safety on a small island. As Subotai turned his army to winter quarters on the shores of the Sea of Ravens, he could not know that on that lonely island the Shah died in poverty and despair. The vast empire of Shah Mohammed II, the "Second Alexander," now lay at the feet of the Mongols.

Genghis and the main Mongol army were encamped on the plains of Nasaf, south of Samarkand, a pleasant mountain plateau with woods, orchards, and cool mountain breezes. During the two years since the invasion of the Shah's empire had begun, the Mongols had won a series of uninterrupted victories, captured the major cities (including the capital), and through a policy of cruel slaughter had laid waste one of the Muslim world's most beautiful and sophisticated areas. Still, the only parts of the vast Khwarizmian Empire that were effectively conquered were the provinces of Transoxiana, the northeastern segment of the empire. The rest, the area to the north, Afghanistan to the east, and Khorassan proper to the west, all remained intact and under at least the tentative control of the old regime. The conquest of these areas remained a vast and dangerous undertaking under any circumstances, more so given the circumstances in which Genghis Khan found himself.

The problem was manpower. Genghis had attacked the Shah's empire with approximately 100,000 to 150,000 troops. Although victorious in almost every battle, the need to assault fortified cities had cost the Mongols severely. Subotai's army, camped on the flats of the Caspian shore, numbered 30,000 men, and Genghis had just dispatched his two sons with a force of

50,000 to continue operations in the north. The tribal contingents, most particularly the Uighurs and Almaliks, had asked permission to return home, and Genghis was disposed to grant the request because reluctant soldiers were likely to be of little use. Outside of Samarkand, then, the main Mongol army numbered perhaps no more than 40,000 to 50,000 troops to carry out further conquest of the Shah's empire. Genghis worried about the manpower reserves available to his enemy. Jalal ad-Din, the Shah's son (and an able military commander), was already raising armies in the east. If the western provinces raised new armies from their enormous manpower base, the Mongols might find themselves trapped between two powerful armies moving against them in coordinated operations. Under these circumstances, Mongol discipline, speed, and maneuver might not suffice, placing the army at grave risk of defeat.

The Mongol intelligence service kept a close eye on Jalal ad-Din and developments to the east. But they knew nothing about the west. Only Subotai and his officers had traveled there, making them the only ones in a position to answer the khan's questions. One day an arrow messenger arrived in Subotai's encampment on the Caspian with instructions that Subotai was to return to Samarkand by order of the khan. Riding from horse station to horse station, sometimes tied to his saddle to ward off exhaustion, stopping only for short periods to eat, Subotai the Valiant, Genghis Khan's greatest general, covered the 1,200 miles from the Caspian shore to Samarkand in little more than a week.

The Arab chroniclers captured the conversation between Subotai and the great khan. Subotai told the khan of the wealth and power of Khorassan, its great cities and powerful fortresses. Its lands stretched from Herat to Merv and further west to Nishapur; but the land was harsh, and it was scarcely possible to travel along the edge of the desert where it was days between settlements or sufficient wells. After listening intently, the great khan asked, "How long would it take a Muslim army to march from Iraq to Khorassan?"

According to the Arab chroniclers, Subotai replied that, "in summer, it would not get to Khorassan at all . . . for the sun burns the grass and dries up the rivers."[15] In winter, Subotai continued, no army could move either, for forage was thin and the Muslim horses were unlike the Mongol ponies that knew how to scrape away the snow with their hooves to get at the grass beneath. Therefore it was only possible for a Muslim army to come to the aid of Khorassan in the autumn or spring, and even then it would require a very large baggage train to do it. Both the size and the ponderously slow rate of march of such an army would make it incapable of surprise attack. The Mongols would see it coming with plenty of time to spare. That is, of course, if it came at all. Subotai told the khan that he had ridden from one end of Khorassan to the other and had seen no evidence of anyone trying to raise an army. What forces there were, and they were substantial, were shut-up in their garrisons and showed every intention to remain so. Unlike in the east where Jalal ad-Din was rallying his people, there was no leadership in the west to carry out the same task. Subotai was confident that no army would come to the aid of Khorassan.

If Subotai's information was correct, the great khan had nothing to fear from a relieving army from the west, and thus no fear of it linking up with Jalal ad-Din in the east. Therefore, he turned his attention to the task of conquest and sent his armies against Khorassan and Afghanistan. The two theaters of operations were 600 miles apart, a vast distance for any European army (and, perhaps, most armies of the modern period as well), but one easily traversed by the Mongol armies. With their speed and the ability to communicate daily by arrow messengers, the two armies, though dispersed for separate campaigns, would never be out of contact. Moreover, the distance between them was not so large that if the need arose, either army could quickly come to the aid of the other and recombine into a single force. And so, Genghis Khan began to complete his conquest of the Khwarizmian Empire.

In the spring of 1221, the Mongol army crossed the Amu Darya and began the conquest of Afghanistan and Khorassan. The Mongol columns swept down on Balkh. Although it had surrendered earlier to Subotai, this did not protect it from total destruction. All the inhabitants were massacred and the town was burned. Genghis then dispatched Tuli to take Merv, which also capitulated. Once again, the entire population was slaughtered. Tuli sat on a golden chair on the plain of Merv and watched the mass executions. Men, women, and children were separated into separate "herds" and given over to the various Mongol battalions and were beheaded. Tuli then attacked Nishapur. It was outside Nishapur that Toguchar, the son-in-law of the khan, had been killed fighting as a common soldier after having been relieved of his command. In revenge, Nishapur was taken by storm and destroyed. Toguchar's widow presided at the massacre of the inhabitants. To guard against deception, the corpses were beheaded, and the heads of men, women, and children were stacked in separate piles; "even the dogs and cats were killed."[16] The Mongols then attacked Herat, whose garrison resisted but whose citizens, hoping for mercy, threw open the gates. This time Tuli spared the civilian population, but slaughtered the Khwarizmian garrison to the last man. His campaign over, Tuli joined Genghis, Jagatai, and Ogedai, who had just captured Urgench.

The Mongols now crossed the Hindu Kush and attacked Afghanistan, taking the city of Bamiyan. During the attack, the khan's favorite grandson, Mutugen, was killed. In revenge, no plundering was permitted; everything was destroyed. No prisoners were taken, and "every living creature was massacred."[17] Further to the east, Jalal ad-Din had taken refuge in Ghazni, in the heart of the Afghan mountains, where he raised a new army. At Perwan, just north of Kabul, he defeated a Mongol army corps. Furious, the khan marched on Ghazni but bypassed the city in pursuit of Jalal ad-Din. After a long chase, the Mongols caught up with the Khwarizmian prince on the banks of the Indus River where, in November of 1221, they trapped his army and cut it to pieces. Jalal ad-Din himself escaped, however, and sought refuge at the court of the Sultan of Delhi.[18] Jalal ad-Din's family had fallen into the hands of the Mongols, however, and all the male children were killed. News of the Mongol defeat at Perwan had reached the rear of the Mongol advance, and several cities revolted against the Mongols. Ghazni, Herat, and Merv all felt the full weight of Mongol vengeance. All were destroyed and what was left of the populations slaughtered or deported. It was with incredible cruelty that the Mongols subdued the great empire of the Khwarizmian Shah.

Subotai took no part in these battles and returned to his camp on the Caspian. During his meeting with the khan, Subotai told him of reports he had obtained from the Kipchaks of a land beyond the Caspian where "narrow-faced men with light hair and blue eyes" dwelled. He proposed to the great khan that he, Jebe, and their force of 20,000 men be permitted to embark upon a long reconnaissance ride around the Caspian Sea, returning to Mongolia through the land of the Kipchaks. Genghis thought the idea a good one, and gave his permission with the instructions that Subotai was to return to Mongolia within three years. In the late autumn of 1220, Subotai and his troop of Mongol cavalrymen began what was to become the most remarkable cavalry raid in military history.

5 THE GREAT CAVALRY RAID

E ncamped along the Caspian flats, Subotai began planning the first Mongol military campaign against the West in the late summer of 1220. Subotai's army comprised 25,000 to 30,000 men and although the dashing Jebe commanded one of the *toumans*, overall command rested with Subotai. It had been Subotai's idea to undertake a great cavalry ride around the Caspian Sea, and the mission was to conduct a reconnaissance-in-force from the area of the newly conquered Khwarizmian state westward as far as was practicable to go. The object of the operation was to gather information for the Mongol intelligence service and to assess the military capabilities of the armies of these strange lands. As documents would later reveal, Subotai was already planning a campaign for the Mongol conquest of Europe.

Looking for a suitable place for a winter encampment, Subotai had probed north along the Caspian shore crossing over the high steppes of northwest Persia and into the province of Azerbaijan making directly for Tabriz, the wealthiest city of the province and the capital of the Turkish governor of Azerbaijan. Subotai threatened to burn the city unless the governor delivered large amounts of silver, clothes, and horses. The governor thought it best to comply, and provided the Mongols with large stocks of booty and military supplies. With winter (1220–1221) drawing near, Subotai moved his army north and east to where the Kura and Araxes rivers emptied into the Caspian. Here, on the Moghan steppes, the winter months are quite mild, and the Mongols passed January building up their horses and preparing for the coming campaign.[1] The Mongol army had been increased by the recruitment of several thousand "wild Kurds," as Subotai referred to them.[2]

In February 1221, Subotai's army began its march around the southern end of the Caspian Sea. Map 5.1 portrays the Mongol area of operations. Subotai's army moved along the banks of the Kura River through the great valley at whose western terminus sat the city of Tiflis (modern Tbilisi) that guarded the approaches to the pass over the Caucasus Mountains. Given the nature of Subotai's mission, a reconnaissance-in-force, it is by no means clear that he intended to engage the Georgians in battle and may have only been seeking a safe passage over the mountains.[3] But the Mongols' reputation had preceded them, and Subotai's threat to sack Tabriz probably convinced the Georgian king, George III Lasha (The Brilliant) that he had to deal with the Mongols on the battlefield or suffer the same fate as the governor of Tabriz. The Georgian army was noted for the quality of its fighting men and weapons and possessed a 30,000-man king's guard of Cuman cavalry. When reports reached the king that a Mongol army was marching up the Kura River through the Cuman plain, George and his army of 70,000 mounted knights set out to intercept it.

The two armies drew up opposite each other for a set-piece battle (Map 5.2). The Georgian cavalry opened the battle with a mass attack (1) against the Mongol center. Subotai ordered his light archer cavalry to sweep across the enemy front unleashing volley after volley of deadly arrow fire; the iron armor-piercing tips of the Mongol arrows took a great toll on the knights. (2) Despite heavy losses, the Georgians pressed the attack, while the Mongols gradually retreated before the enemy advance, drawing the mounted knights after them, until the Christian army was spread out across the plain atop (3) exhausted mounts. Subotai had anticipated the Georgian tactics and positioned fresh mounts for his soldiers in a wood to the rear of the battlefield. Now the Mongols mounted their fresh horses and launched a devastating (4) counterattack. Preceded by a storm of arrow fire, this time the Mongol heavy cavalry, aboard their new mounts, struck the enemy formation and drove a wedge into the Georgian army. The Georgian army broke and ran as the Mongol wings closed in and around the main body. With little hope of holding his ground, the king fled along with those knights whose horses could still stand the pace. A few brave knights made a stand on the road to Tiflis, but were quickly overrun and slaughtered by Jebe's cavalry. For two weeks, George and the survivors of the army awaited the attack on the city itself. It never came. The Mongols had disappeared.[4]

Subotai had withdrawn his army to the south, back down again, into Persia and the province of Azerbaijan. The battle had been a victory, but

Map 5.1   Mongol Theater of Operations

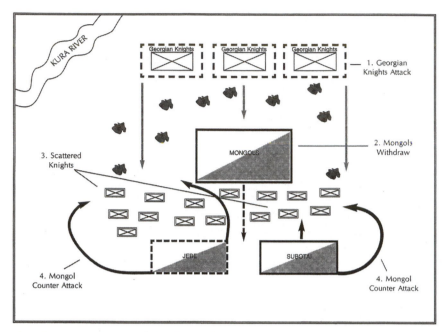

Map 5.2   First Battle of the Kura Plain

fighting it at all had been a mistake. The Mongols' goal was to cross the Caucasus and reach the Russian steppes beyond. If they had to fight a pitched battle all across Georgia to accomplish this, their soldiers would be in no condition to make the passage across the Caucasus, Europe's highest and most difficult mountain range. Subotai's plan had been to carry out raids against soft targets as they advanced, increasing their store of horses and booty which they would need to purchase allies and safe passage once on the Russian steppe. They had neither the time nor the manpower for an attack against a fortified city like Tiflis. So Subotai refused to attack the Georgian capital, and withdrew the army to the south, where it raided Persian towns to replenish supplies and horses expended at the battle on the Kura plain.[5]

Next, the Mongols attacked Maragha using their familiar tactic of pressing Muslim prisoners into the front of their attack formations. On March 30, 1221, they captured the town, slaughtered the population, and carried off as much booty as they were able. The year before, Subotai had extracted a ransom from the city of Hamadan in return for not attacking it. This time the city fathers refused to pay a second ransom, and the Mongols attacked Hamadan with a vengeance. But the inhabitants did not give in without a fight and resisted the Mongols hand-to-hand in what turned out to be a terrible street battle. Once in control, however, the Mongols responded with a massacre of the population. As Subotai's army turned north once more, the smoke from the ruins of one of Persia's finest cities rose behind them.[6]

In late autumn of 1221, when winter was already beginning in the foothills of the Caucasus and no medieval European army expected to take the field, Subotai and the Mongol army advanced westward into Georgia once more. This time they raced up the coast of the Caspian toward Derbend, the powerful city lying between the western shores of the Caspian and the Caucasian foothills of Dagestan. Here the great fortress guarded not only the city and its harbor, but also the Gate of Gates, the pass of Bab al-Abwab that led through the mountains into the steppes. Given the time of year and the indirect route that Subotai had chosen to make his advance, it is likely that he had hoped to avoid any contact with the Georgian army. If so, he had been disappointed. Probably believing that the Mongol failure to attack Tiflis earlier in the year meant that he had defeated them on the battlefield (despite his flight from the fighting!), King George arrived with a large army to block the Mongol advance. Subotai's attempt to accomplish a passage of the Caucasus without a fight had failed, and he turned to deal with the Georgians.

The battle was fought on much narrower ground than before, on a battlefield tight against the foothills of the Dagestan range, the last foothills of the Caucasus barrier. A range of steep hills ran along the east side of the battlefield. In between was a narrow pass, in which Subotai had positioned 5,000 men under Jebe's command. Map 5.3 portrays the positions of the various elements during the battle. Having learned from their first experience with the Mongols, this time the Georgian knights retained their packed formations as they moved deliberately against the Mongol line. (1) They moved slowly, staying out of reach of the Mongol arrow fire. Subotai seems to have been content to permit this impression in the mind of the Georgian commander, for as his waves of light cavalry bowmen swept repeatedly across the enemy front, their arrows continued to fall short of the Georgian ranks. Subotai had instructed his archers not to take too high a toll of the advancing Georgian knights. As the Georgians advanced, Subotai retreated further until, their main body now opposite the opening of the pass, the Georgian ranks were struck in the flank by Jebe's ferocious attack. (2) Taken by surprise in the flank, the Georgians wheeled to meet the attack, convinced that Subotai would continue his retreat. Fixed on dealing with Jebe's attack, the Georgians became fully engaged. (3) Now Subotai halted his retreat, wheeled around, and drove straight at the exposed flank of the Georgian army, striking it hard and rolling it up, driving right through it and shattering the cohesion of the Georgians in a single overwhelming attack. (4) Under assault from two directions, the Georgians collapsed and began to flee. The king and his bodyguard escaped, but the rest of the Georgian army was annihilated.[7]

With this second defeat in less than a year at the hands of the Mongols the Georgian army—one of the finest in Christendom—had ceased to exist, leaving Georgia completely without defenses. George the Brilliant died leaving only an infant son and the crown passed to his sister, Rusudan, the "Maiden King." It was Rusudan who wrote to the pope that:

> a savage people of Tartars, hellish of aspect, as voracious as wolves in their hunger for spoils as brave as lions, have invaded my country. . . . The brave knighthood of Georgia has hunted them down out of the country killing 25,000 of the invaders. But alas, we are no longer in a position to take up the Cross as we had promised your Holiness to do.[8]

There would be no Georgian military contingent for the next Crusade. The Georgians had lost more than 100,000 men-at-arms in their two battles against Subotai's army. For years afterward, with no army to protect them, Georgia was ravaged continually by brigands and bandits.

Subotai and his army rode into Derbend and invested the fortress where Rashid, the Shah of Shirvan, had taken refuge. Subotai intended to cross the Caucasus in the dead of winter and needed provisions and guides to see him and his army across the mountains. Subotai had no interest in a long siege of the city. Rashid and the Mongols came to a quick agreement, in which the Mongols would leave the city untouched and move on across the mountains while Rashid agreed to provide fodder, supplies, food, and, most importantly, guides to lead the Mongols through the mountains. But the Muslim Shah was no fool, and he personally selected the guides from among those who could be trusted to follow his instructions. They were told to lead the Mongols over the mountains, but to do so by the longest and most difficult route possible. The Shah also sent secret messengers over the mountains by the shortest route to sound the alarm on the western steppes. Subotai may well have suspected some treachery. He selected one of the chosen guides and had him beheaded as a warning to the others. As events turned out, the guides remained loyal to their instructions and led the Mongols over a tortuous route.

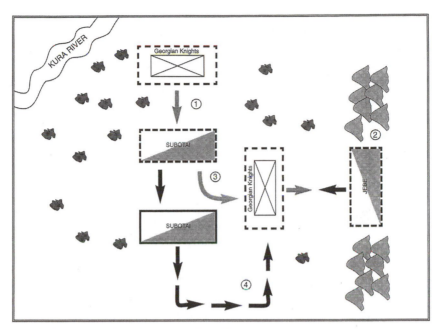

Map 5.3   Second Battle of the Kura Plain

The crossing of the Caucasus was costly; the Mongol catapults, mangonels, and much of their baggage had to be abandoned in the snow. Hundreds of Mongol soldiers froze to death. Jebe must have been reminded of his earlier trek across the Tian Shan Mountains into the Fergana Valley during the Khwarizmian war. And the similarity did not end there. As the Mongols forced the pass and started down the glaciers of the Caucasus between the precipitous dark rocks to reach the gorges along which raging torrents led into the valley of the Terek River, Subotai found an army of 50,000 men awaiting them, deployed for battle on the plain below. Jebe, too, had been confronted in this manner when he stumbled into the Khwarizmian Shah's army waiting in the Fergana Valley. Exhausted by the trek and with ranks thinned by death, Subotai's army faced an enemy more than twice its size, fully equipped, and deployed to block the Mongol exit from the narrow mountain pass that severely restricted the Mongol ability to maneuver.

The army confronting the Mongols was a coalition of mountaineer peoples of the Caucasus. Counted among them were Lesghiens, Tcherkesses, and Alans, this last a people of Iranian-Scythian stock who were Orthodox

Christians.[9] Leading the coalition were the Kipchaks, or Cumans, who were related to the Kanglis that the Mongols had slaughtered in the Khwarizmian campaign. The royal Georgian bodyguard that the Mongols had recently annihilated had also been composed of Cuman cavalry. But there was more to the Cuman resistance than blood revenge. The Cumans were the traditional plunderers of the Russian steppe between the Volga and the lower Danube. A pagan people, they regarded this land as their own preserve of plunder and they regarded the Mongol presence as a threat to their monopoly. The Cumans had also convinced the Bulgars and Khazars to join their alliance, and the Cuman chief, Kotian, had sent this large army under the command of his brother, Yuri, to block the Mongols' avenue of advance.[10]

The Cuman chief was aware of the Mongol approach over the mountains, having been informed by one of Rashid Shah's messengers, and had raised and deployed a massive army to destroy the Mongol invaders. For one of the few times in his long military career, Subotai found himself trapped in circumstances that he did not anticipate. He could not retreat, returning over the mountains, for to do so would mean abandoning his mission and probably having to face a Muslim army raised by Rashid Shah waiting at the other end. With no means of retreat and the terrain depriving him of the ability maneuver, Subotai ordered his exhausted army into a frontal attack. Although the Mongols pressed the attack fiercely, there was no hope of breaking such a great mass of armed men. Subotai was forced to retreat back into the steep hills and to take up defensive positions with his archers behind the rocks. Yuri, Kotian's brother, and his son, Daniel, commanded the coalition of tribes and refused to be drawn into a Mongol ambush. Nor did they risk their troops with pointless attacks against the Mongol positions by making easy targets for the Mongol archers. Instead, the Cumans and their allies camped on both sides of the exit to the pass and settled down to await either the Mongol withdrawal back over the pass or death by starvation and exposure.

In a classic example of the importance of diplomacy to military victory, Subotai dealt with the problem by guile. He sent emissaries to the Cumans with bribes of gold and horses, pointing out that the Cumans and Mongols were brothers of the steppes who had no reason to war with each other. The only true enemies of the Mongols were the Muslims and Christians. The Cuman contingent took the bribe, and stole away in the night, leaving the remaining tribal contingents at the mercy of the Mongols, who promptly slaughtered them. But Mongol scouts followed the Cumans, and when they divided their army into two contingents, each going its separate way, Subotai and Jebe closed fast after the main body, caught up with it, and slaughtered them. The treasure and the valuable horses were recovered and all of the Cuman prisoners were executed. The Mongols then attacked Astrakhan and sacked the city. The road to Russia now lay open.

Subotai rested the army and replenished his supplies. His army was now numbered fewer than 20,000 men, but the Mongols were at last free of the towns and mountains and at home on the open steppe. Determined to continue the reconnaissance that was their main mission, Subotai divided his army. Subotai, with 10,000 men, rode southwest to reconnoiter the coast of the Sea of Azov and make certain that the Cumans had not managed to find allies in the area to help launch an attack on the Mongols again. Jebe, with the rest of the army, rode west to find the Don River and wait for Subotai to arrive. On this ride around the Sea of Azov Subotai first encountered men from Western Europe. They were merchants from Venice who had built a small trading station on the shore of Azov. Subotai recognized these merchants as a valuable source of intelligence about the West and invited them into his camp, where he entertained them lavishly.

The Venetians were eager to establish relations with the Mongols, whom they recognized from their military equipment, their fine Chinese-silk shirts for example, as not being a barbarian people, and answered Subotai's questions and those of his intelligence officers. Subotai had equipped his army well for its intelligence-gathering mission. Among its staff officers were Chinese scholars who had made detailed maps of the areas already traversed. From the information gathered from captured prisoners and scouting parties, maps of the lands that lay to the front were drawn. Even provisional maps of Hungary, Poland, Silesia, and Bohemia were designed, based on information provided by the Venetians. These officers even took a crude census of the area, made surveys of the crops and yields, and even compiled notes on the climate. Subotai's army traveled with doctors, diplomats, and a corps of interpreters that included an Armenian bishop. Indeed, the Muslim merchants in the Mongol baggage train were so efficient that they were already selling cheap copies of the Bible to the local Russians, a fact that surely impressed the Venetian merchants.[11] By the time the Venetians left, they had signed a secret treaty with the Mongols in which traveling Venetian merchants would send back detailed reports of the economic strength and military movements in the countries they visited. In return, the Mongols promised to destroy all other trading stations in the lands in which they rode, leaving Venice with a monopoly wherever Subotai's men went.[12] During the autumn and early winter of 1222, Mongol scouts and reconnaissance parties moved over the Don and Dnieper Rivers and conducted forays into the Crimea and along the Dniester River gathering information and reporting on troop movements.

Having learned that his brother and his son had died at the hands of the Mongols, Kotian took the remnants of the Cumans northward, seeking refuge in the Russian duchies of Kiev and Chernigov. Kotian sought to convince the Russian princes of the need for concerted action against the Mongols. For almost a year, his pleas fell on deaf Russian ears; for the Russians themselves had been the victims of Cuman raids for decades and were not displeased with the treatment these brigands had received at the hands of the Mongols. But once news reached Kiev that the Mongols were marching along the banks of the Dniester River and laying waste the farms and towns there, some Russian princes were willing to listen to the Cumans' pleas. Foremost in support of the Cuman cause was Mstislav the Daring, Prince of Galicia, who had preserved his own lands from Cuman predations by marrying one of Kotian's daughters. Mstislav agreed with Kotian's estimate of the strategic situation and convinced the other princes to assemble an army and meet the Mongol threat before it was upon their lands. Mstislav and his son-in-law, Prince Daniel of Volynia, were the first to assemble their troops. They were soon joined by the contingents of Prince Oleg of Kursk and the princes of Kiev and Chernigov along with Grand Duke Yuri of Suzdal, who sent a contingent under the command of his nephew, the Prince of Rostov. When combined, the Russian army numbered over 80,000 men. Slowly, the various Russian feudal armies began to converge on Subotai and the Mongol army.

The ominous movement of the Russian armies was detected by Mongol scouts. Subotai had expected reinforcements from Juji, who was campaigning north of the Aral Sea. But news arrived by messenger that Juji was ill, and that no reinforcements would be forthcoming. The Mongols were positioned on the east side of the Dnieper River near the great bend, southwest of the city of Kursk. The Russian armies were converging on a prearranged rendezvous point on the island of Khortitsa, in the Dnieper River. The army from Kursk had already crossed the Mongol path to the front and the Cumans were advancing over the steppes toward the Mongol rear. The armies of the princes of Kiev and Chernigov were moving down the river from the north. In the south, the princes of Galicia and Volynia transported their armies in 1,000 boats down the Dniester and the coast of the Black Sea in an attempt to land behind the Mongol armies. If Subotai did not move quickly to the east, he risked being caught in the Russian multi-pronged advance.

Once more, the Mongols tried to use diplomacy to shatter a superior coalition of armies. Mongol ambassadors were sent to the Prince of Kiev with the message that the Russians had nothing to fear from the Mongols. The Mongols had come only to destroy the Cumans, a common enemy of the Russians as well. Further, the Mongol armies were marching east, away from Russia, not in the opposite direction toward the Russian cities. The Prince of Kiev refused to fall for the ruse and had the Mongol ambassadors executed. He was somewhat surprised, however, when the only Mongol reaction to their execution was to send another ambassador with a formal declaration of war. Mongol military etiquette required, wherever possible, a declaration of war before beginning hostilities.

To avoid being cut off by the movement of the Russian armies, Subotai and Jebe continued to move east, away from Russia. They left behind a rearguard of 1,000 men under the command of an officer named Hamabek to report on enemy movements and delay the Russians as they crossed the Dnieper. As the main body of the Mongol force moved away more quickly than the Russians could follow, the vanguard of the Russian army under Mstislav the Daring reached the river opposite the Mongol rearguard in the midst of the chaos created by the arrival of the other armies. It was now clear that no one had been given overall command of the Russian forces, and each retained the right to act as he chose. Arguments over what to do broke out as the Mongol rearguard waited patiently on the opposite bank. At last Mstislav crossed the river in boats with, perhaps, as many as 10,000 troops. The Mongol arrows took a heavy toll as the rearguard held its ground. Eventually Russian numbers proved too much, and the rearguard was overrun and slain to a man. Its commander, too, was killed. Mstislav, encouraged by his victory, took off in hot pursuit of the Mongol army while the rest of the Russian contingents crossed the river and, one by one, struck out after Mstislav.

For nine days, the Russian army pursued the Mongols as they retreated north of the Sea of Azov with the Russian contingents becoming strung out behind one another over a distance of almost fifty miles. Now, however, the Mongols were riding over terrain they had previously reconnoitered, and Subotai used his knowledge of the terrain to his advantage. On May 31, 1223, the Mongols halted on the west bank of the Kalka River and, with the river to their backs, turned about and formed for battle, waiting for the Russians to arrive. As the Russian vanguard under Mstislav rode into the valley, they were confronted by the Mongol army in battle formation (Map 5.4). (1) Without waiting for the rest of the contingents to catch up or even to send messengers to the rear to inform his commanders of his plan of action, Mstislav the Daring ordered his Galicians and the Cumans into a frontal cavalry attack. (2) The trailing combat units of the princes of Kursk and Volynia, hurrying to catch up, also moved into the attack.

The Russian attack was very much uncoordinated. The Mongol light cavalry engaged by riding backward and forward in the path of the Russian attack, concentrating their arrow fire with typically deadly effect. The arrow fire created a gap between the Cumans and the Galicians. The Mongol light cavalry broke off the attack as clouds of black smoke from Mongol firepots drifted across the battlefront. (3) As the Russians became disoriented by the smoke and movement, the Mongol heavy cavalry suddenly appeared and charged into the gap between the two contingents.

The shock was tremendous, and the Cumans broke in terror and fled to the rear. Meanwhile, the Russian contingents from Kursk and Volynia, who had been late into the assault, separated to allow the Cumans to pass between them. But the Mongol heavy cavalry was close in pursuit of the Cumans and rushed into the gap, attacking the Kursk and Volynia contingents with great ferocity. The army from Chernigov, not even aware that a battle was in progress when they approached the battlefield, collided head on with the fleeing Cumans. As quickly as the Cumans smashed into his forces, the prince of Chernigov found himself under attack by the pursuing Mongol cavalry. (4) Suddenly, the wings of the Mongol army closed around the smashed contingents, cutting off their retreat. Surrounded, the Russian army was ravaged by volley after volley of archery fire coupled with periodic pulses of heavy cavalry attack. As the Mongols began to systematically slaughter the Russian army, some of its remnants, led by Mstislav the Daring, managed to break out of the ring. Fleeing to the rear, they rode straight into the last Russian contingent to reach the battlefield, the Prince of Kiev and his army. (5) The defeat turned into a rout, and the Russian army fled. The troops of the slow-moving prince of Suzdal-Vladimir had managed to advance no further than the city of Chernigov by the time the battle of the Kalka River was over.

At the end of the day, a Mongol army of 18,000 men along with its 5,000 Brodniki allies had slain over 40,000 Russians, including six princes and seventy nobles. Then the lethal Mongol pursuit began. For 150 miles, until the defeated army reached and crossed the Dnieper, the Mongol cavalry

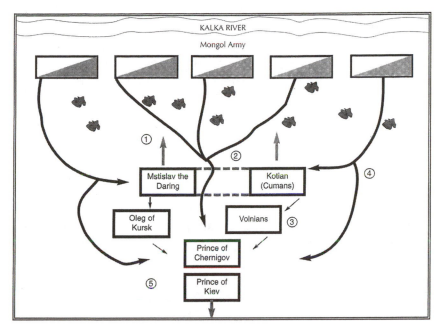

Map 5.4   Battle of the Kalka River

slew the remnants of the Russian army. The Prince of Kiev, to his credit, covered the withdrawal of the rest of the army across the Dnieper with strong resistance from his 10,000-man contingent, fighting from a fortified camp on the riverbank. Within three days, however, the Mongols successfully stormed the camp and slaughtered the Kiev contingent, killing 10,000 Russians.[13] For the murder of the Mongol ambassadors, the Prince of Kiev was suffocated to death inside a box. Mongol tradition forbade the shedding of royal blood except in battle. All princes, Mongol or otherwise, according to Mongol law were to be either strangled or suffocated.

The way to all Russia now lay open. Subotai crossed the Dnieper and ravaged the countryside, massacring the local population as a reminder of Mongol power. Then a messenger arrived from the Great Khan with instructions to find Juji's army, link up with it, and defeat the Volga Bulgars. Somewhere near Tsaritsin (modern Stalingrad, now Volgagrad) Subotai's army crossed the Volga and marched northeasterly toward the Bulgars.[14] Shortly thereafter, the exhausted Mongol army under Subotai linked up with Juji's army. At a battle on the Kama River, the Bulgars were defeated, but not before the Mongols had suffered an initial defeat in a well-planned Bulgar ambush.[15] The details of the ambush and the later Mongol victory have not survived. Never a people to forget treachery, the Mongols recalled that the eastern Kanglis Cumans had joined with their fellow Cumans to oppose the Mongol crossing of the Caucasus passes a year earlier. The Mongols attacked the army of the Kanglis Khan near the Ural Mountains. In a lightning campaign, the Khan was killed in battle, his army massacred, and his people terrorized and forced to pay tribute. With this last act of vengeance, the Mongol army turned eastward and headed for the main army where Genghis Khan awaited them on the banks of the Syr Darya River. Map 5.5 shows the general route of Subotai and Jebe's great cavalry raid.

Subotai and Jebe had been gone for three years. Jebe died of fever and never reached the Mongol capital. Subotai left behind scores of spies and secret messengers to provide regular reports on all that went on in Russia and Europe. This information was passed to the Mongol intelligence service, which began compiling dossiers on the various European countries and the political and religious rivalries that divided them. Subotai's reconnaissance into Russia was history's longest cavalry ride, over 5,500 miles in about three years. On that ride Subotai and Jebe won over a dozen battles against superior numbers. Perhaps most important, the information gained from the reconnaissance showed that a vast corridor of steppe land ran from Mongolia to Hungary, and along that corridor the armies of the Mongols could move faster than any army in the world. Subotai's great cavalry raid had been a reconnaissance mission, and his army was far too small to attempt conquest. The next time the Mongols came to the West, they did so in force.

In 1227 Genghis Khan died. His choice of his son, Ogedai, as his successor was ratified by the great *Kurultai* held in Karakorum in 1229. By 1234, Mongol rule in Persia was consolidated, and the Chin Empire in northern China was formally annexed. In that same year, the Kurultai decided to engage in four military operations simultaneously. By this time, the war against the Sung in southern China was already underway. By some estimates, this war cost the Chinese ten million dead, a truly terrible loss of life. Korea had been occupied in 1231, and a Mongol army was needed to suppress a large-scale revolt on the peninsula. A third army was operating in Persia, threatening the area around the Caucasus and the Black Sea as a prelude to eventual operations in the Middle East. A fourth army was poised to invade Russia and then Central Europe.

The Great Khan assembled an army of 150,000 men, the size decided upon as a result of an estimate provided by his intelligence officers. The

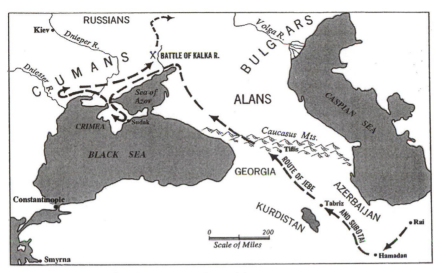

Map 5.5   Route of Subotai's Cavalry Raid

report also concluded that a campaign to subdue Europe from the Urals to the Atlantic would require approximately sixteen to eighteen years to complete successfully. At the head of this great Mongol army, Ogedai appointed the grandson of Genghis Khan, Batu. While Batu lent credibility and prestige to the adventure, he was too inexperienced to command an army of such size on an operation of this scale and complexity. To guide Batu in his decisions, Ogedai sent along Subotai the Valiant as his chief—of staff and operational field commander. Ogedai had placed the mission of conquering the West in the hands of the boyhood friend of his father, the only remaining *orlok* of the khan, and the Mongols' ablest and most experienced general.

6 THE ATTACK ON THE WEST

Russia on the eve of the Mongol invasion (1236) was a nation of vast forests, swamps, and plains inhabited on the eastern periphery by a number of semi-barbarian and pagan tribes—the Cumans, Bulgars, Khazars, and others. Within Russia proper, there was no national authority. The country was divided into a number of small and weak principalities. Feudalism reigned, with little in the way of enlightenment from the West. The country was in continuous turmoil over localized feudal wars and foreign invasions. Between 1054 and 1224, Russia had endured eighty-three civil wars between principalities, and it had been invaded no fewer than forty-six times from east or west.[1]

For the Mongols, the strategic key to conquering Russia was to attack each principality quickly and in isolation to prevent the formation of any coalition of forces sufficiently large to oppose their military operations. Russia was a country almost without serviceable roads that could be used as axes of advance. Enormous distances, severe climatic conditions, and the scarcity of stone account for the fact that ballasted roads appeared in Russia only shortly before the railroads.[2] In summer, huge holes usually blocked what few roads there were, and in spring and autumn, the notorious Russian "roadlessness" (*rasputitsa*) made it nearly impossible to travel for at least a month in either season.[3] For these reasons, and the fact that European feudal armies were rarely prepared or equipped to fight in winter, the Mongols launched their attack in winter, when the frozen rivers, streams, and marshes presented no obstacle to Mongol horse mobility and, in fact, enhanced it.

THE RUSSIAN CAMPAIGN

Military operations began in 1236–37 with the objective of destroying the Bulgar kingdom near the junction of the Volga and Kama Rivers, and neutralizing the nomadic tribes east of the Volga River. Map 5.1 (in the previous chapter) depicts the Mongol theater of operations during this campaign. Subotai sent his soldiers to subjugate all the peoples east of the Volga between the Kama River and the Caspian, destroying their towns, slaying the inhabitants, and taking many of their men prisoner. By one account, the destruction of the capital city occasioned the death of 50,000 people.[4] To the south, Mongol columns attacked the Cumans, many of whom were taken as prisoners while others fled over the Volga. They found refuge in Hungary, where many converted to Christianity.[5] There were two reasons for Subotai's attacks. The first was to clear his left flank of potentially hostile peoples who might be tempted to attack his lines of communication. Second, the Bulgars and Cumans were nomadic people with long traditions of horsemanship and fighting on horseback. These tribal warriors were impressed into the Mongol army. During the summer and fall of 1237, the defeated young men of these border tribes were trained in Mongol methods of war and integrated into the Mongol formations under the careful eye and command of Mongol officers. These contingents swelled the size of the Mongol army to almost 200,000 men. In December 1237, in the dead of winter, Subotai led the Mongol army across the frozen Volga River and advanced into Russia.

The easiest route to Western Europe was directly west, through the steppes between the Volga and the Carpathian Mountains. But an advance along this route might provoke the southern princes to retreat north into the trackless wilds and make common cause with the northern Russian princes. There the Russians could obtain reinforcements from the north and, once the Mongol army was strung out along the plain, attack in considerable strength along the Mongol flank and rear. To secure their vulnerable right flank and protect against attack, Subotai led the Mongol army northwest, into the forest regions, directly at the northern principalities, determined to begin his campaign by breaking the power of the northern Russian princes. Informed by intelligence reports, Subotai was relying upon the inability of the Russians to form a common front against a rapid operational advance.

The Russians of the northern principalities showed an even greater incapacity to unite against the common enemy than had the southern principalities had at the time of the battle of the Kalka River, and the Mongols picked them off one at a time. The Mongols first stormed the town of Riazan, like most Russian fortified places, protected only by wooden palisades, which crumbled quickly under the pounding of Mongol artillery after a bombardment of only five days. Three days before Christmas, Mongol horsemen entered the city and turned it into a slaughterhouse. Men were hunted through the red snow and the alleys of the town and impaled upon stakes to wriggle out the tragic end of their lives. Priest and monks who had shut themselves up in their churches and monasteries were exterminated like sheep, as were the women who had sought sanctuary with them. The slaughter at Riazan was so horrendous that a chronicler reported that, "no eyes remained open to weep for the dead."[6] Another chronicler wrote, "Some were impaled, or had nails or splinters of wood driven under their fingernails. Priests were roasted alive, and nuns and maidens ravished in the churches in front of their relatives."[7] The city leaders had sent messengers to Yuri of Vladimir with appeals for help, but he did nothing. The lesson of the Kalka River battle had been completely forgotten.

The Mongols moved on to Kolomna, which suffered the same fate as Riazan. Only fifty miles from Moscow, the Grand Duke of Suzdal was finally moved to action and ordered his vassals to assemble an army on the Sita River. But it was too late. Subotai moved quickly against Moscow, storming and destroying Rostov and Yaroslavl along the way. The Mongol columns followed the frozen rivers from one citadel to the next. Moscow was then a small town and citadel located on the steep cliff above the Moscow River, where it joins the Neglinnaya. Although it was not yet a great city, it was sufficiently important to have a substantial garrison. The Grand Duke hoped that the city would hold out long enough for the Russian armies to assemble on the Sita and come to its aid. The Novgorod Chronicle tells us that it was a vain hope: "And the men of Moscow ran away, having seen nothing."[8] The Chronicle also tells us that somewhere along the Kolomenka River, a Russian army, perhaps a relief column moving towards Moscow, suffered "a bitter and violent death." The Grand Duke was frightened now, and, leaving his wife and family in Vladimir, he rode out to join the army assembling on the Sita. Subotai's intelligence officers must have learned of his departure, for with Moscow in flames, the Mongols turned back and rode the hundred miles to Vladimir without pause and brought the city under assault. A Mongol detachment was sent to follow the Grand Duke and report on his movements. A large Mongol force then moved the twenty-five miles to the north to storm the city of Suzdal, whose defenses the Mongols carried in a single day.

The attack on Vladimir began on February 7, 1238. Two days later, the Mongols stormed all four gates at once and carried the defenses. Again, the slaughter commenced. The Mongols burnt the wooden palisades of the town and slew the archbishop, who had taken refuge in the cathedral. The Grand Duke himself had now joined the assembled Russian armies on the Sita River. But while Subotai maneuvered to the north, the Russians did nothing, content to rely upon their superior numbers and await the Mongol attack. The Mongols, however, were nowhere to be found. And then, at the end of February, the Russians sent out a reconnaissance force of 3,000 men to locate the Mongols.[9] To their horror, the Russians discovered that they were surrounded by Subotai's army, which formed up outside the Russian camp to offer battle. It was winter, and the battlefield was deep with snow. The feudal levies marched out of their log and dirt fortifications slowed by the snow's depth, only to be struck by the firepower of Mongol arrows that crippled them from a distance. In short order, the Russian army died in the blood-stained snow, its best warriors fighting hand-to-hand until the end. The Grand Duke was killed and decapitated.

Having destroyed the Russian army, Subotai moved quickly to the north, burning what was left of Rostov, Yuriev, and Yaroslavl on his route to join Batu, whom he had sent ahead in command of half the army to threaten Novgorod, Russia's wealthiest city. Along the way, Batu had destroyed Dmitrov and Tver. By March of 1238, much of northern Russia was in smoking ruins. In less than two months, twelve walled Russian cities had been destroyed and Mongol advanced units were only a hundred miles from Novgorod itself.[10] Batu's columns reached Torzhok first, and brought it under attack. The city put up a fierce defense that lasted more than two weeks. By the time Batu was ready to continue his march toward Novgorod, the spring thaws had melted the snows, swollen the rivers, and turned the whole countryside around Novgorod into a swampy morass. Fearing that they might be caught in the spring floods, Subotai ordered his army to pull back.[11] The Mongols were within sixty miles of the city. The garrison at Novgorod represented no significant threat to the Mongol flank and the northern Russian principalities were neutralized. Subotai turned his armies southward, toward the steppe pastures of the Don basin and the western

Ukraine. The Mongol losses had been significant, and Subotai replaced them from among captives taken from the Cumans and other steppe peoples of the area. For the remainder of the year the Mongol army rested and replenished itself for the coming campaign against Europe.

In late fall of 1240, the Mongol advance began again, this time striking at the southern Russian principalities. Chernigov was the first to fall to the Mongol attack, followed by Pereyaslav, both of which were destroyed. Russian resistance remained only local, with no effort to organize a national defense. The peasant levies and the city militias led by their small feudal aristocracies of knights took the field only to be routinely slaughtered by the superior Mongol military machine. By November, the Mongol advance columns had reached the outskirts of Kiev. That month, Subotai ordered his main army across the frozen Dnieper River, arriving outside the gates of Kiev and bringing it under attack in early December. Kiev, the center of the Orthodox faith and one of the great cities of Western religion, was a city of churches and monasteries; one of the few Russian cities with a wall of stone instead of a wooden palisade. The Mongol artillery bombardment focused its fire upon the Polish Gate, the one section of the defensive wall that was made of wood. Under intense fire, the gate collapsed and Mongol heavy cavalry rushed through it into the city. The Russians mounted a gallant defense and the Mongol penetration was stopped. The assault was resumed the next day, and on 6 December of 1240, Kiev was taken in fierce hand-to-hand fighting. The city was put to the torch and its people massacred. The destruction was so great that when a traveler passed by the ruins of the city six years later, he described it as having only a few hundred huts with the ground still littered with "countless skulls and bones of dead men."[12]

After the fall of Kiev, the Mongol armies continued their advance against little more than token opposition. Within three weeks, Subotai's army had reached the western border of Russia. Volynia and Galicia were attacked and overrun. The cities of Kremenets, the Volynian city of Vladimir, Cherven, Przemysl, and Galich were attacked, captured, and plundered. At the same time, many smaller towns were wiped off the Russian map forever. The leaders of the Russian nobility had already fled to Poland and Hungary, leaving their vassals to their fate.[13] With Russian military resistance now completely crushed under the Mongol heel; Subotai turned his attention to the West. He assembled his commanders near Przemysl and outlined his audacious plan for the conquest of Europe.

THE CAMPAIGN AGAINST HUNGARY

At this point in the campaign, Western Europe was only dimly aware of the Mongol threat. The Cuman nation, the most numerous nomadic people on the Russian steppe, fled in front of the Mongol advance into Hungary. There they offered to serve the Hungarian king, Bela IV, and convert to Christianity in return for his protection against the Mongols. Knowing that the conversion of 200,000 pagans to the Church would be well received in Rome, and that the addition of thousands of Cuman cavalrymen to his own army would increase his military power, Bela accepted. The Cumans brought with them tales of Mongol military prowess and massacre, increasing the knowledge of the Mongol threat in the West.

Subotai rested his armies across the river from Kiev. Thirty thousand men were detached from the main army to control the conquered regions and protect the Mongol lines of communication. In December of 1240, Subotai began the next phase of the European campaign. Western Europe was unable to mount any coordinated military plan to meet the Mongol threat despite adequate warning provided by the Cumans. The Holy Roman Emperor, Frederick II, and Pope Gregory IX were locked in a war of their own for earthly supremacy, and neither could spare any troops. The principalities of Lithuania, Sweden, and Poland were small politico-military units that jealously guarded their prerogatives to the point that military cooperation was impossible. The degree of suspicion and fragmentation was evident from the fact that, while the Mongols were assembling for an attack on Hungary after having just ravaged Russia, the Lithuanians and Teutonic Knights were attacking Russian cities in the hope of profiting from the Russian tragedy. Europe was simply incapable of any kind of concerted political or military action. The Mongol intelligence service had correctly gauged the political weakness of Europe.[14]

Subotai had 120,000 men at his disposal to carry out the invasion and conquest of Hungary. Map 6.1 depicts the various elements and routes of advance of Subotai's armies as they moved against Hungary. The Mongol army concentrated across the Vistula at Halicz in early January 1241. The target was the Hungarian capital of the twin cities, Buda and Pest. As the Mongol army advanced toward its objective, Subotai expected that the army of Bela IV would move out in advance of the city to do battle. If it did, Subotai would have the opportunity to destroy the last significant armed force between the Mongols and Central Europe. He divided the invasion force

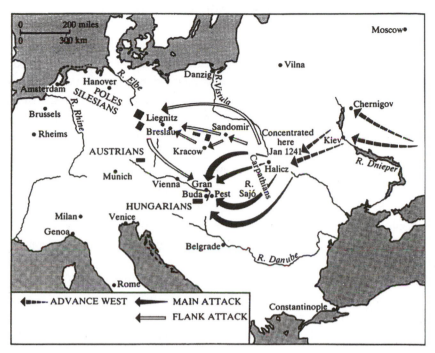

Map 6.1   Subotai's European Campaign, 1240–1242

into four columns, each of which was to cross the snow-filled passes through the Carpathian Mountains in the dead of winter and in different places. Baidar led the northernmost penetration, while Batu moved his troops through Galicia. Kuyuk's columns swept through Moldavia and Transylvania to the south, and Subotai swept furthest south, through the Mehedinti Pass and came at Buda and Pest from the south. If things went according to plan, the Mongol army would suddenly appear outside the Hungarian capital ready to do battle with Bela.

The main objective was Hungary. But Mongol columns moving through the Carpathians onto the grassy plains would be at grave risk to an assembled force deployed on the plains of Poland. The European armies of the Polish and German states were intact, and represented a major threat to the Mongol right flank. To protect the main operation in Hungary from any surprise attack from the north, Subotai dispatched a force of 30,000 men under Kaidu, grandson of Ogedai. Its mission was to strike into Poland, Bohemia, and Silesia, engaging European forces in these areas as a distraction from the main attack falling on Hungary. In March of 1241, somewhat ahead of the other columns, Kaidu's army advanced toward the Polish frontier.

Kaidu's army struck directly for the army of the Polish king of Cracow, Boleslav V ("The Chaste"), which had taken up position at Sandomir. As the Mongol columns approached, Boleslav withdrew to Moravia, taking his family and treasure with him. Command of the army was left to Vladimir, the palatine of Cracow. What remained of the army melted away as the various sub-vassals and princes fled with their contingents. Vladimir, accompanied only by the house guard, stood against the Mongols at Chmielnik, thirty miles in front of Cracow, and there he was crushed. The Mongols entered Cracow on Palm Sunday, March 24, and found the city deserted. The population had fled to the forests. The Mongols put the city to the torch.

The Mongol army crossed the Oder River near Raciborz, and Kaidu divided the army into two columns. Two *toumans* struck for Breslau, while the remaining touman moved through Poland, and then swung west through Lithuania, East Prussia, and along the Baltic coast of Pomerania. The Mongol task force killed, burned, and looted as it went. Refugees fleeing to the West carried with them horrible tales, including the belief that the Mongol army numbered 200,000 men. Meanwhile, Kaidu's army reached Breslau and concluded that the stone fortifications were too difficult to overcome. Kaidu bypassed Breslau and swept into Silesia. Mongol reconnaissance units reported the first signs of organized resistance to the Mongol invasion, and Kaidu prepared to find and destroy the enemy army.

THE BATTLE OF LIEGNITZ

Henry the Pious, Duke of Silesia, assembled an army to save Christian Europe from the Mongol horde. At the same time, King Wenceslas of Bohemia marched northward with an army of 50,000 men to join Henry. Kaidu determined that he could not permit the two armies to link up, and moved rapidly toward Liegnitz to find Henry's army and take the battle to it before Wenceslas could arrive. Henry did not know when reinforcements would arrive, and was concerned that unless he moved his army into open ground, he would be trapped in the city and be unable to deploy effectively. Around 9 April of 1241 (historians cannot agree on the exact date of the battle), the two armies met on a wide plain—*die Wahlstadt*, or "chosen place"—a few miles south of the city.

The Duke of Silesia divided his army into four "battles" or combat contingents. However, these were usually irregular in size, composition, and national or local origin. A group of "battles" formed the line. Command was assigned on the basis of birth, not because of proven competence, as in the Mongol armies.[15] A Mongol commander might be anywhere within a battle formation, directing his troops. A European army commander, by contrast, often fought alongside their men in the thick of battle where he was easily identifiable (and thus could be deliberately killed), and unable to respond to larger developments in the fight. The first contingent consisted of Henry, a retinue of handpicked troops from the knights of Poland and Silesia, and some mercenaries. The famed Teutonic knights made up the second "battle" and remained under the command of their *Landmeister*, Poppo of Osterna. Clad in their hauberks covered with white mantles with black crosses emblazoned on the front and their full-face helmets, the Teutonic knights were the elite force of the European army. The third contingent was a group of Polish knights drawn from the lesser Polish nobility and the fourth "battle," probably infantry, was described in the chronicles as "an army of gold-digging peasants from Silesia." Facing the Europeans across the open plain was the 20,000-man army of Kaidu Khan.

The details of the battle, especially with regard to the timing of specific battle movements, are not entirely clear, so that only a general picture of events can be reconstructed here (Map 6.2). Early in the battle, one of Henry's cavalry brigades, perhaps the Polish knights under Boleslav, undertook an attack against the Mongol center to begin the usual hand-to-hand mounted combat. (1) The Mongol light cavalry quickly encircled the brigade and brought it under murderous arrow fire. Boleslav held his ground for only a short time. Once he realized that no other contingents were coming to his support, he ordered his knights to break out of the Mongol encirclement and fall back. (2) Henry now committed the main body of his cavalry forces to an attack on the Mongol center. This second charge by the second and third brigades was mounted under Sulislav and Meshko of Opole. A wild melee ensued in which the Mongol cavalry was pressed back until it broke into a headlong retreat. (3)

Thinking that the Mongol center had given way, Henry and his own contingent, along with the rest of the Silesian cavalry units, were eager to meet the enemy with lance and broadsword and gave chase only to ride into the Mongol trap. It was the old Mongol trick, the feigned retreat, designed to separate the enemy cavalry from its infantry and to loosen the enemy's

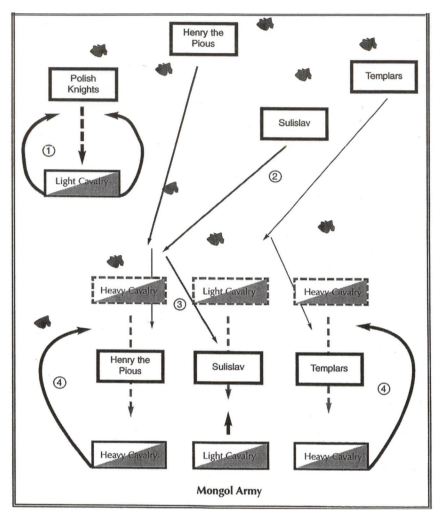

Map 6.2   Battle of Liegnitz, 1241

packed formations during the chase. The Silesians' extended and disordered lines were suddenly met with fresh cavalry attacks on the wings from more Mongol light cavalry, who had waited for the knights in ambush and now proceeded to decimate them with volleys of arrow fire. Suddenly, behind Henry's entrapped squadrons, the battlefield filled with black smoke from Mongol firepots, further confusing the trapped cavalry and separating it farther from the infantry. As the Mongol heavy cavalry closed the circle around the knights and began to shoot them down at close range, the light cavalry darted in and out of the smoke destroying the infantry with arrow fire. (4) Whenever the Mongols found that their arrows could not pierce the armor of the knights, they simply shot their horses out from underneath them. Afoot, the dismounted knights were easy prey for the Mongol heavy cavalry who ran them down with lance or saber, with little danger to themselves. It was in such a dismounted group that the Knights Templar made a determined stand, only to be killed to a man.[16]

In the dreadful slaughter that followed, almost the entire army, including the *Landmeister* of the Teutonic knights, was slain. Henry himself was decapitated. His headless and naked body was found on the battlefield. His wife recognized the body as belonging to Henry because of the six toes on his left foot. The Mongols tallied the body count by cutting off the right ear of every dead enemy soldier. Nine large sacks of victims' ears were carried away from the battlefield in the Mongol war wagons. The Grand Master of the Templars wrote to King Louis IX of France, telling him of the slaughter of his comrades in the battle. He also noted that no army of any significance stood between the Mongols and France. This was no exaggeration. All Europe was now defenseless against a Mongol attack aimed at the heart of Western Europe. But the battle of Liegnitz, while a catastrophe for the Europeans, had been only part of Subotai's plan, designed to preempt any flank attack against the main Mongol army which had already forced the Carpathian passes and was now marching into Hungary, covering 40 miles a day in the snow. His mission accomplished, Kaidu recalled his column that had been ravaging the Baltic coast and turned his army southward to join with Subotai's armies that were poised to destroy the Hungarian army deployed on the Sajo River.

If the Mongol army was truly the most organized and combat efficient army that the world had seen in almost a thousand years, it was also true that the armies it fought during its European campaigns—Russian, Polish, German, and Hungarian—were hardly a match for the Devil's Horsemen. All of the Mongol enemies in the West were feudal societies, and the raising of an army under the feudal system, whereby barons and other vassals were obliged to provide their king with soldiers in return for their estates, worked well enough, as long as the war was close to home and didn't last very long. No feudal army had a logistics system of any worth, so that provisioning and maintaining an army in the field was a very difficult task. Although the main arm of these feudal armies was heavy cavalry, when compared to the mobility and flexibility of the Mongol cavalry, European cavalry had lost many of its military capabilities. The knight's armor had grown heavier over the centuries, leaving the cavalry charge as the only real tactic of the mounted knight armed with the lance. But the weight of the knight, armor, and horse removed any flexibility in deployment, leaving the knight capable of a single charge in one direction, straight ahead. The European heavy cavalry was simply no match for its Mongol counterpart.

A singular weakness of the feudal armies was that their contingents were raised individually as contributions from the barons and other vassals. As such, knights had no training in anything but individual combat. They had no experience in fighting as coordinated units. Moreover, the emphasis on the personal combat skills of the knight provided no opportunity to develop those personal skills required to lead men in battle. Although there were distinctions in social and military rank, feudal armies had no formal chain of command that could compel unit commanders to conform to the general battle plan, assuming there was someone around to draft one in the first place. As long as feudal armies fought one another, none of these obvious weaknesses had necessarily been fatal. However, when matched against an army of the sophistication and combat lethality of the Mongols, the armies of feudal Europe were hopelessly outclassed.

From the battle of Adrianople to the eleventh century, the defensive armor of the European knight gradually grew heavier and bulkier, until, by the time of the Crusades, it deprived the knight of considerable bodily movement and any possibility of rapid attack. During the Crusades, the old heavy armor was gradually replaced by the hauberk, a coat or tunic of chain mail. Chain mail had been known in the West since the time of Rome, but it had gradually disappeared in Europe during the dark ages. It remained popular in the Middle East, however, and the Crusades brought western armies into contact with this type of armor again. Chain-mail armor had quickly been adopted by Western armies, and it had become the standard armor from the eleventh to fourteenth centuries, when it was gradually replaced by plate armor. The hauberk was made of individual metal links tempered in turnip juice to make them supple. The entire mesh suit was riveted or sown to a leather or cloth tunic, providing full body and sleeve protection to the wearer. By 1250, mail mittens were added to protect the hands, and even mail breeches were introduced to protect the legs. Less expensive versions of shorter and sleeveless mail shirts emerged called *haubergeons*, and they were sometimes worn by infantry. Also in common use by foot troops (and poorer knights) was the *gambeson*, a thickly padded, quilted coat that worked well in resisting sword cuts. During the Crusades, it became common practice to wear a gambeson over the chain mail. Saracen historians noted the tendency of arrows to stick in this overcoat without penetrating the mail underneath, thus giving the impression of padded pincushions. The heat of the Middle East led Crusader knights to copy the Saracen custom of wearing a loose gown over the hauberk to protect the chain mail from becoming hot from the sun.

A typical helmet of this period was the conical metal skullcap, with a nasal piece to protect the face. Gradually, nasal and chin pieces grew to envelop the entire face, until the helmet evolved into a cylindrical, flat-topped helmet, with a slit for the eyes. At the same time, the pointed bassinet helmet came into use, with the added advantage of having a removable face-plate or visor to allow for breathing when not in battle. Underneath the helmet, the knight wore a coif or chain mail hood that draped over his neck and shoulders, providing good protection. A full suit of armor weighed about 150 pounds, but the weight was relatively well distributed over the entire body. The flexibility of the chain mail permitted fairly good range of movement, so that the knight could bring his weapon to bear with some effectiveness in close combat. Robert Jean Charles, a French expert in medieval armor, asserts that a knight in chain mail was really no heavier "than horsemen in Napoleonic days whose steeds had to carry a considerable weight in arms and field supplies as well as the rider."[17]

Much mythology surrounds the subject of the knight's horse. The weight of the knight's armor was not—at least until the fourteenth century, when plate armor became common—so heavy as to present a real problem for a normal horse to carry. Except in Germany, where knights wore much heavier armor and required stronger horses, the knight's battle steed was only slightly larger than average. As the efficacy of chain mail made the sword ineffective in mounted combat, by the end of the twelfth century the mounted knight turned to the lance as the primary combat weapon. This new style of combat brought about the development of higher saddle brows and cantles to support the horseman. The high, curved saddles also protected the soldier's hips and belly. When in the attack, the knight stood up in the stirrups and leaned against the front of the saddle in order to throw his entire weight and that of his cantering horse behind the thrust of the lance. A 1,800-pound knight and horse moving at twelve to fifteen miles per hour could produce more than 200,000 pounds of kinetic energy at impact.

The experience of the Crusaders in the Middle East against horse archers and disciplined infantry operating in concert with cavalry produced a change in European tactical doctrine. As the knight's horse became more vulnerable to arrow attack, it became necessary to find some way to protect the horse. Beginning originally with cloth padding, and ending two centuries later with almost full armor plate, the warhorse evolved into a fully armored tank. Armoring the horse solved only half the problem, however. Saracen infantry used their lances to pull the Crusader knights off their mounts. At the same time the introduction of newer types of infantry weapons—the crossbow, halberd, scimitar, and several variations on the pike—placed the mounted knight at greater risk than ever before. To neutralize this threat, the mounted knight took to dismounting after the initial cavalry charge and fighting on foot. When this solution was applied against the heavy cavalry lancers of the Mongols, however, their ability to rapidly change direction and bring their lances to bear while remaining on horseback turned dismounting into a dangerous practice.

Although the sword was an object of almost mystical veneration among medieval warriors, by the eleventh century it had ceased to be the main combat weapon. In response to the effectiveness of chain and, later, plate armor, the sword became long and tapered with an almost needle-like point. The purpose of the design was to allow the swordsman to get the sharp point of the sword under the arm, in between the shoulder and arm joint, or in some other area where the sword might penetrate the armor. The decline in the effectiveness of the sword led to the greater use of smashing weapons—maces, hammers, axes—that could be used to strike the armored knight with the intention of breaking the bones underneath the chain mail.

All of the major European armies that the Mongols fought were essentially armed in a manner similar to that just described. Because the military structure of the feudal period was a reflection of its social structure, all European armies were similarly organized, trained, and armed, and in all these armies, the armored knight was the centerpiece of combat power. At the same time, however, there were significant differences in the stress placed upon other fighting arms by a given army, as well as their respective abilities to assemble and arm significant numbers of fighting men. As was usually the case, these factors were a result of the degree of organizational articulation found in the social orders of the respective states.

The Russian army, at the time of the Mongol attack in 1237, was very similar to the Frankish army of the eighth and ninth century and consisted of two separate bodies: the *druzhina* of the princes and major nobility, and the city militia. The druzhina was a corps of horsemen, who followed their feudal lords into battle clad in chain mail and armed with heavy lances, shields, and swords. These *comitati* were supposed to serve as shock brigade, and the Russian princes relied heavily upon their maneuverability and tactical skill to carry the day.[18] The second body of troops was the city militias, which were only called to arms in emergencies or for major campaigns. There was no definite contingent of militia troops. Presumably, every able-bodied man in the city who could be provided with weapons and horse was expected to serve. Some of Russia's larger cities could field 15,000 to 20,000 militiamen.[19] In times of great emergency a general levy of infantry could be drawn from the peasantry, or *smerdi* (literally "the stinking ones").[20] The weakness of the Russian army was that the heavy cavalry of the druzhina were few in number, while the infantry were not well armed and had no military training. Russian infantry carried the axe, spear, and the usual retinue of agricultural implements, to the general neglect of archery. City militiamen on horseback were by no means good horse warriors and, in any case, no match for the Mongols. The small size of the Russian cavalry corps led it to rely upon auxiliary cavalry troops, most often Turks or Cumans. Russian armies had only primitive logistics trains and usually lived off the countryside as they passed through. Russian tactics were almost completely uninformed about maneuver warfare, and usually drew the army ready for battle in front of a wooden stockade surrounding the camp. The cavalry anchored the center of the line, with infantry on both wings and in the rear to act as a reserve. The infantry's basic role was to defend the cavalry, and only the cavalry engaged in the attack.

The Polish army encountered by the Mongols in 1240 was an army consisting almost entirely of cavalry lancers. One reason for this was that, while the free yeomanry was still numerous in Russia, in Poland, the free peasant had all but disappeared into serfdom. Land ownership in Poland was somewhat fragmented so that the landowning aristocracy, the *noblesse*, was relatively large. Ownership of even a few acres entitled the farmer to bear arms. The Poles, unlike their neighbors the Russians and Magyars, were a nation of lancers. The rich nobles served in complete mail and with an excellent horse while the poorer landowners fought in a leather coat on a lesser horse. Horse archers and foot infantry were nonexistent. The only meaningful military distinction was between heavy and light cavalry.

Of some military significance was the fact that neither the Russians nor the Poles constructed fortified cities of stone, and the Western military art of castle building had not taken root in either country. The most important nobles lived in wooden mansions protected by a wooden palisade, and with a few exceptions—Kiev being most importantly—neither country had any cities with substantial fortifications constructed of anything but wood. The Mongol siege experts and artillery made short work of these flimsy barricades. It was the Polish and Russian custom not to defend cities. Rather, during invasion the populace usually abandoned the cities and hid in the substantial forests until the invader had gone.

The German army and the armies of the cities across the Oder presented a far more difficult challenge to the Mongols. Perhaps nowhere in Europe were the military arts of the medieval period more acutely and expertly developed than in Germany. German knights wore more armor, rode larger horses, and trained more often as a fighting force. It had been Germany, after all, that had given birth to the Teutonic Knights, celibate warrior-monks devoted to the spread of Christianity by the sword. These were tough, disciplined, well trained, and highly motivated professionals. Besides excellent armies, German cities were routinely fortified with walls of stone, moats, and towers. Local constabulary forces tended to be excellent, and the German could be depended upon to fight fiercely for his feudal lord or churchman. Even for the Mongol army, a campaign conducted against the German army on its home ground was a difficult task.

The Mongol campaign against Central Europe brought them into contact with perhaps the second best army of the region, the Hungarians. The Hungarians were a warlike nation. They had been steppe-dwelling horse archers before settling in the Danube basin less than two centuries earlier. They were well led and accustomed to the tactics of mobile warfare as practiced by the Mongols. The Hungarian aristocracy had adopted the Western style of warfare and armament that went along with the feudal social order. Accordingly, the centerpiece of the Hungarian army was the Western-style armored knight armed with the lance and trained in the cavalry charge. Most of the peasant levies fought on horseback, armed with bow and saber. The firepower, mobility, and endurance of the Hungarian army were somewhat inferior to the Mongols, but of all the armies in Europe, the Hungarians were the most formidable in battle, especially on the open plain.

The military capability of the armies of Europe during the time of the Mongol invasions (1237–1241) left much to be desired. In a set-piece battle, the Mongol army had a number of advantages in firepower, mobility, training, command, and endurance. On the other hand, the European armies had the advantage of fighting on their homeland for a cause, usually buttressed by religious faith. The Mongol armies were far from home and dependent upon long lines of supply and communication. The ability of the Mongol army to move within the theater of operations depended upon maintaining an excellent reconnaissance capability. No Mongol had ever been to Central Europe, and the army's commanders had to continually feel their way in strange territory. The Mongol army succeeded because it was superior in the operational arts, not because the inherent structure of its army was superior. As with armies throughout history, victory depended less upon the nature of the army *per se* than upon what a talented commander could do with it. And in the person of Subotai, the commander of the invasion of Europe, the Mongols had a commander far superior to any European commander who had taken the field in the preceding two centuries.

BATTLE OF THE SAJO RIVER

While Kaidu Khan was ravaging Poland and defeating King Henry at Liegnitz, the four columns of Subotai and Batu's main force worked their way through the snowy passes of the Carpathian Mountains in an attempt to gain the Hungarian plain. By early March, the columns of the main Mongol army had overcome token resistance and broken through the last of the fixed Hungarian defenses at the Carpathian passes. The southern columns, smaller than the center columns, had begun to raid the outlying districts in an attempt to distract King Bela's attention from the larger force that was marching on Buda and Pest along the central axis of advance. Bela took the bait and sent a small force under the palatine Denis Hedevary to block the Mongol advance on the southern axis. The Mongols easily brushed it aside.

In early March, King Bela conceded that the Mongols had breached the Carpathians in force and called a council of war in Buda, 200 miles behind the point of the Mongol advanced columns, to consider how to stop the Mongol advance. While the council was in session, Bela received word that the advanced guard of the Mongol army had already reached the banks of the Danube outside of the city of Pest. As Bela tried to decide on a course of action, the Mongol columns were arriving at their assembly point a few miles north of Pest. Bela believed that the swollen Danube and the strong fortifications of Pest were sufficient to stop the Mongol advance until he could assemble his army. He did not think it strange, however, that the Mongol commanders made no effort to ford the river or lay siege to the city of Pest. Within two weeks, by the first few days of April, Bela had assembled his army of nearly 100,000 men, and had begun his march eastward to repel the Mongol invaders.

As Bela's army advanced, the Mongols slowly withdrew in front of it. The cautious pursuit of the Mongol army went on for nine days. During the morning of the tenth day, Subotai crossed a stone bridge over the Sajo River and encamped his army a few miles beyond the stream. The Mongols left only a token detachment to guard the bridge. Subotai was tempting Bela to cross the Sajo, where he could attack and push the Hungarian king back into the swift waters of the swollen river. Bela refused to take the bait, and halted on the west bank of the river. Prior to going into defensive positions, Bela drove the small Mongol detachment from the bridge and established a significant bridgehead on the east bank of the Sajo to defend the bridge from Mongol counterattack. The main body of Bela's army remained on the west bank and encamped for the night. The stage was set to Subotai's liking for the decisive battle of the Hungarian campaign. In the strategic view of the Mongols, both of their flanks were secure, the lines of communication were secure and within easy reach, the main army was concentrated on the selected battlefield, and the enemy was completely isolated.

Chroniclers of the battle of the Sajo River recorded that Bela's army was perhaps 100,000 strong, and that it certainly outnumbered the Mongol army. Comprising numerous contingents of armored knights, the major part of this army of former Magyar nomads was horse archers thoroughly familiar with Mongol tactics. But the morale of the army was low, as a consequence of rumors of the Mongol ravaging of the countryside. The news of the disaster at Liegnitz had also been discouraging. The Hungarian king was not popular with all his knights, many of whom thought him too great a friend of the church. Two of Bela's most able and trusted commanders—Ugolin of Kolocza and Matthias of Gran—were archbishops. Bela's disposition of forces on the west bank also left much to be desired. Although the Sajo is fordable in a few places, Bela guarded only the bridge. His camp was pitched too densely and too close to the river, with the effect that his army occupied too narrow a front. Batu is said to have pointed out this essential mistake to his generals. "They are crowded together," Batu said, "like a herd of cattle in narrow stalls, with no room to move about."[21] Subotai followed Napoleon's dictum never to stop an enemy commander from making a mistake. The final flaw in Bela's position was that he did not use his light cavalry or horse archers to establish flank security up and down the riverbank, thus leaving both his flanks exposed.

Just before daylight, Batu attacked the bridgehead held by the Hungarian detachment on the east side of the river. The defenders found themselves under fire from the thirteenth-century equivalent of an artillery preparatory bombardment. The Mongols brought up seven siege engines, probably ballistae, and bombarded the bridgehead with firebombs and other noisemakers. The object of the bombardment was to focus the attention of the enemy commander on the point of attack, and in this case, it succeeded very well. The defenders, stupefied by the noise and death from the artillery, were suddenly attacked by squadrons of Mongol cavalry who quickly overwhelmed them. The artillery fire shifted to long range, and the Mongol cavalry crossed the bridge under cover of something akin to a rolling barrage. Although surprised by the attack, the Hungarian commanders rallied their troops and sallied forth from their camp to engage the Mongol force pouring across the bridge. A bitter battle ensued, in which the Hungarians held their own and forced the Mongols to give ground. Suddenly, it became alarmingly apparent that the engagement was only a Mongol holding attack.

In the spring, the rivers of Hungary run swift and deep in full flood and are significant obstacles for even modern combat engineers. But the audacious Subotai had found a way to cross. Some miles downstream from the bridge on the Sajo there was a small peninsula surrounded by swamp that protruded into the river. It was very unsuitable for the crossing of any sizeable force. With an outlet to the west bank of the river barely two miles wide, no more than 2,500 horsemen could have ridden abreast on that peninsula. Subotai had used the cover of night to move three full toumans (30,000 men) across the Sajo and out over the narrow peninsula and on to the west bank. He then assembled his force, turned northward, and arrived on the battlefield while the main Hungarian force was strongly concentrated opposite the bridge to meet the Mongol holding attack.

Subotai's sudden flank attack rolled into the Hungarian army, almost shattering it in a single stroke. To their credit, the Hungarians did not panic, but withdrew into their camp. The Mongols moved up their siege engines, and for several hours, they bombarded the Hungarian army with stones, arrows, and burning naphtha. Batu increased the pressure on the bridge, and Subotai launched two columns to encircle the camp. The crafty old general deliberately left a gap between the arms of the wings of the pincer, and it soon became apparent to the Hungarians that there was a gap to the west

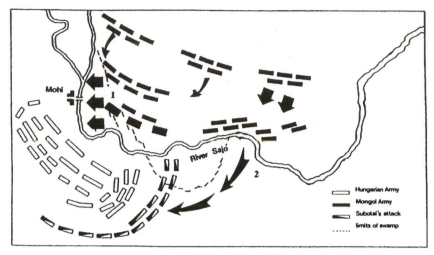

Map 6.3   Battle of the Sajo River: Subotai's Night Crossing

that might lead to safety. The Mongol assault increased in intensity. At first, a few horsemen galloped through the gap to safety. Soon a stream of men was pouring through the gap, as the Mongols did nothing to stop the withdrawal. Only a handful of Knights Templar held their ground—they died to a man. As the defense of the camp collapsed, more and more soldiers rushed through the gap. Military discipline broke down and many threw away their armor and weapons.

As the column of defeated knights grew longer and more dispersed, the Mongols sprang the trap. Mounted on fresh horses, Mongol detachments suddenly appeared from nowhere on both sides of the column. Subotai had planned to catch the enemy in the pursuit on open ground; his cavalry units had done just that. The Mongols began cutting down the exhausted and defenseless Hungarians, hunting them down when they tried to escape, and burning villages in which they sought to take refuge. The horrible butchery lasted for two days, and, when it was over, bodies littered the road to Pest "like stones in a quarry." Between 50,000 and 70,000 Hungarian soldiers died in the disaster. Emperor Frederick wrote of the losses that day, "*Fere extinguitur militia totius regni Hungariae*" ("The entire royal army of Hungary was destroyed").

With the destruction of the Hungarian army, the Mongols controlled all of Eastern Europe from the Dnieper to the Oder, and from the Baltic Sea to the Danube River. In four months, they had overwhelmed Christian armies

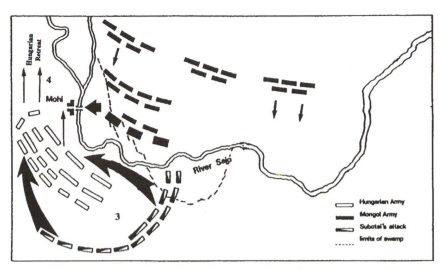

Map 6.4   Battle of the Sajo River: Subotai's Flank Attack

totaling five times their own strength. Subotai consolidated his hold on
Hungary and ravaged the country from end to end, destroying many of its
towns. One estimate placed the loss to Hungary from the Mongol invasion
at fifty percent of its population![22] As soon as the Danube froze over, Subotai's columns crossed the river to the west. Spearheads crossed the Julian
Alps into northern Italy and Mongol reconnaissance columns moved
through the Danube valley and approached the walls of Vienna. The sover-
eigns of Europe were paralyzed with fear and waited helplessly for the arrival
of the barbarians.

As the Mongols reconnoitered Vienna, an arrow messenger arrived from
Karakorum with the news that Ogedai Khan was dead. Mongol law required
that all royal offspring had to return to the capital to take part in the election
of a new Khan. The invading army had three royal princes with it, and Subotai reminded them of their duty. The Mongol columns stopped and turned
eastward, and began the long march back to Karakorum. Their route took
them through Dalmatia, Serbia, and across northern Bulgaria. As they passed
through these lands, they laid them waste before vanishing across the lower
Danube, never to return to Europe. In Russia, the Mongols set up their own
state—The Golden Horde of Batu Khan—and held Russia under their yoke
for almost three centuries. It was from the Mongols, far more than from the
West, that the Czars learned their methods of political rule, in which absolute power was used absolutely.

7 THE MONGOL MILITARY LEGACY

The attack on Western Europe by Subotai's armies ended as quickly as it had begun, so that by the end of 1242, the Mongol armies had retreated to the east, never again to threaten the armies of Europe. The great trauma of the Mongol invasion that frightened the princes and churchmen of Europe to death was quickly forgotten, with the consequence that the European experience of the Mongol armies had no discernible effect on western military practice. Further to the east, however, beyond the Polish border in Russia, the Mongol assault and later occupation of Russia itself shaped Russian politics, military practice, and the national psyche in fundamental and enduring ways. For more than three centuries after the battle of Liegnitz, Mongol armies occupied the Russian heartland, leaving behind a legacy of absolute power used absolutely, so that Russian methods of political rule and notions of authority were strongly influenced by the Mongol occupation. The liberating ideas and ideals of the Renaissance never reached Russia in sufficient force to influence its development.

When, by the sixteenth century, the Russians had finally driven the Mongols from their land, Russia was already hemmed in from the West by other states, prohibiting any expansion in that direction. To the southwest, the Turks held the Balkans. To the west, the Polish state was at the height of its territorial and military expansion. Beyond Poland, the Lithuanians held the marshes and forest areas. In the northwest, Novgorod was still fighting wars with the Germans, while Swedish power held the shores of the Baltic. Even the northern forests were closed to Russian expansion, as the warlike Finns held tenaciously to their ancestral heritage.[1] Unable to expand in any other direction, the Russians pressed eastward, and, over three centuries, recreated the old Mongol empire, this time from west to east. One consequence of this eastward expansion was that it brought the Russian military into frequent contact with the Mongol style of war, as it was still practiced by the ethnic peoples of Central Asia. Russia fought a number of military campaigns against Mongol-style armies right up until the end of the Nineteenth century,[2] with the result that Russian military doctrine and practice was strongly influenced by its long historical experience with the Mongol way of war.

Western European armies and strategists, by contrast, paid only scant practical attention to the lessons that might have been learned from the Mongols. The first European to attempt an understanding of Mongol military methods, equipment, strategy, and tactics was Giovanni di Plano Carpini, who wrote an account of his visit to the Mongol court between 1245 and 1247. His *Historia Mongalorum quos nos Tartaros appellamus* (The Story of the Mongols Whom We Call the Tartars) was published in 1248,[3] and as far as can be discerned, was quietly forgotten, without having influenced European military thought or practice to any degree. Marco Polo, writing of his experiences at the court of Kublai Khan some years later, also produced an analysis of Mongol military practices. It, too, was ignored. There is no evidence to suggest that any military thinker or practitioner in Western Europe ever paid any attention to the Mongol campaigns. Even the West's most renowned scholar of military affairs, Hans Delbruck, writing in his magnificent multi-volume work, *The History of the Art of War*, failed even to mention the Mongols in his analysis.[4] The result of the direct Russian experience with the Mongols and the European ignorance of this experience resulted in a situation in which Russian military thought and practice up to World War II was significantly influenced by Mongol methods and lessons of war, while these methods and lessons remained largely unknown in the West.

As far as the author is able to tell, the first modern military historian to write an analysis of Mongol military methods was a Russian Lieutenant General, Mikhail I. Ivanin (1801–1874).[5] As a young officer, Ivanin had taken part in the Russian campaign against the Khanate of Khiva, fought against the semi-nomadic Uzbeks in Central Asia. During this campaign, Ivanin experienced firsthand the tactics of the Mongols, as practiced by the Uzbeks, and in the same area and under conditions similar to Genghis Khan's Turkestan campaign. This experience seems to have aroused Ivanin's interest in Mongol military methods, and, in 1846, he published *The Art of War of the Mongols and the Central Asian Peoples*.[6] In 1854, Ivanin was appointed Russian commissioner in charge of the affairs of the inner Kirghiz Horde, where he spent several years collecting more information on the military dimensions of the Turkish tribes of Central Asia. Later, he returned to his historical studies, and, in 1875, a revised and enlarged edition of his earlier book was published posthumously. The work was immediately recognized in Russia as an important contribution to military thought and became a textbook for the students at the Imperial Military Academy. As far as can be determined, however, Ivanin's book was neither translated nor read in the West, even as it remained a recommended text in the Russian military academies up through, at least, World War II.

One might have expected that the great trauma of World War I would have stimulated some interest in the West with regard to the Mongols, at least insofar as the tank had raised the possibility of reintroducing mobility to the battlefield. Sir Basil Liddell-Hart considered this possibility in 1927; as he wrote in the chapter on Genghis Khan in his *Great Captains Unveiled*: "Is there not a lesson here for the armies of today? . . . the armored caterpillar or light tank appears the natural heir of the Mongol horseman."[7] J. F. C. Fuller thought the airplane might have the same qualities to an even higher degree. A French military historian, Henri Morel, wrote the first article on the Mongols to appear in the West in 1922. His "Les campagnes mongoles au XIII e siècle," appeared in the *Revue Militaire Francaise* of that year. In the same year, the officers of the Mechanized Brigade were encouraged by the chief of staff of the British Imperial Staff to study the great raids of the Mongols, but little came of it.[8] Between 1932 and 1933, Squadron Leader C. C. Walker contributed a series of articles on Genghis Khan to the *Canadian Defence Quarterly*. These were later collected into a monograph entitled *Genghis Khan* published in 1939. These efforts at bringing the expertise of the Mongol armies to the attention of Western strategic and tactical thinkers were meager enough, and there is no evidence to suggest that any of these analyses were taken seriously or integrated into the curricula of any western military college or school.

World War I had proven the military doctrines that preceded it to be seriously deficient when it came to actual combat, with the result that what had been initially conceived of as a war of mobility quickly degenerated into a war of immobile stalemate and trench battles. This experience led military strategists, between the wars, to rethink their ideas in light of practical experience to discover solutions to the problem of immobility that had characterized the fighting in the Great War. The military thinkers of each of the great powers saw the problem differently, however. For the French, for example, the problem was how to break through the enemy's defensive line and escape the confines of an elastic defense once the attack had begun.[9] The French solution was a new doctrine emphasizing massive firepower, enshrined in the motto "artillery conquers, infantry occupies."

British military thinkers, for the most part, expected the next war to be largely a repetition of the last one, and urged their political leaders to simply remain aloof from future European conflicts.[10] One consequence of this view was the failure of the British army to make any significant doctrinal or tactical changes between the wars. Some military thinkers, B. H. Liddell-Hart and J. F. C. Fuller in particular, criticized the lack of English military thinking with doctrines of their own. Liddell-Hart had suggested that the modern tank was equivalent to the Mongol horseman and, as such, could be used to restore mobility to the battlefield. But Liddell-Hart saw the strength of the Mongol army inhering in a "single arm army," that is, horse cavalry, and suggested that modern armies could rely upon the single arm of mobile armor.[11] This was, of course, a misreading of Mongol military history, for while the Mongol army had indeed relied upon a single arm (horse cavalry), each *type* of cavalry, heavy and light, had completely different tactical functions even if they were utilized jointly. Liddell-Hart's emphasis on Mongol cavalry also led him to neglect the Mongol use of infantry. To be sure, this infantry comprised captured local inhabitants, but it was infantry nonetheless, and it had been used in a manner to support both types of cavalry. In short, Mongol armies had used infantry in concert with cavalry, and, in this sense, had been combined-arms armies. Liddell-Hart also neglected the Mongol use of direct fire, employed by the light infantry to prepare the assault, as well as their use of artillery as preparatory bombardment, oversights which led him to ignore the role of these arms in making his argument that what Britain needed was a single arm army composed largely of tanks. J. F. C. Fuller, by contrast, did understand the Mongol use of preparatory fires and suggested that both the modern airplane and the new self-propelled artillery could serve the same function in modern armies. All of this aside, however, both Fuller and Liddell-Hart were seen as disloyal critics, and neither had any significant impact on the development of British strategic or tactical thinking between the wars.

German military strategists saw the problem of immobility and trench warfare in yet another way. In the German view, the basic problem stemmed from the need to prepare the battlefield with days, sometimes weeks, of artillery bombardment prior to attempting a breakthrough. Long artillery bombardment inevitably made strategic and tactical surprise impossible, making it almost certain that the depth of the defenses or the employment of the elastic defense would quickly contain any breakthrough. The German solution was the new doctrine of Blitzkrieg, which Heinz Guderian summed up in the motto, "surprise, deployment en masse, and suitable terrain."[12] It is sometimes thought that the Russian emphasis on armor and frontline aviation in combat support, which came to characterize the Blitzkrieg doctrine, were copied from the Germans. In fact, it was the Germans who were introduced to Soviet doctrinal concepts, which the Germans then copied. The Rapallo Pact of 1923 between Germany and Russia allowed for the training of German officers and the testing of German equipment on Russian soil. This situation brought German military planners into contact with the newly developing Red Army. The Germans were greatly impressed by the new operational doctrine implemented by General Mikhail Nikolayevich Tukhachevsky (1893–1937), which emphasized the employment of forward aviation in concert with rapidly moving tank columns. They were further impressed by the advanced design of Soviet tanks, and subsequently incorporated some Soviet designs in their own tanks. The shortcoming of the Blitzkrieg doctrine was that it was a purely tactical doctrine. Western military thinking between the wars was still heavily influenced by the Napoleonic concept of war, namely, that a series of large-scale battles and victories would force the enemy to surrender or begin peace negotiations. Western thinking focused upon tactical applications and lacked any strategic dimension, insofar as it failed to attend to the circumstances of greater scope and scale apart from the battlefield itself that might bring about a strategic decision. Indeed, all the Western doctrinal solutions to the tactical problem of immobility lacked this strategic dimension.

Only the Soviets saw the problem correctly. In the Soviet view, the problem was not achieving a breakthrough against in-depth defenses, something that had been done many times during the course of the war. Nor was the problem only one of surprise, which under most conditions was a temporary circumstance that was quickly lost if the offensive could not be sustained. To the Soviets, the problem of modern warfare came down to *the seizure and maintenance of the offensive over a long period of time,* so that the continuing battles at the tactical level were but means to the larger strategic goal of destroying the enemy's will to resist across the whole spectrum of his forces. In short, the Soviets were the only ones to develop a concept of war that incorporated both strategic and tactical dimensions. This is the doctrine of Deep Battle, incorporated in the Field Regulations of 1936. It was the brainchild of Marshall (after his promotion) Tukhachevsky, Chief of Staff of the Red Army.[13]

The central concept of the Deep Battle doctrine was the seizure of the offensive across the whole range of the enemy's tactical deployment; conducting long-range attacks deep in the enemy's rear areas against his troop concentrations, road junctions, communications, cities, supply depots, etc. The goal of Deep Battle is to paralyze the enemy's ability to concentrate in force, always forcing the enemy to react rather than plan and act in the offensive.[14] This is, of course, the Mongol practice of war in the strategic sense, a sense that also guides its tactical application. The Soviet emphasis on surprise, maneuver over long distances, maintaining the offensive, and striking the enemy in depth all have their origins in the Mongol experience; likewise the Soviet use of fire to prepare for the assault, the reliance on tank columns, and the stress upon maneuver, encirclement, and annihilation of the enemy wherever he can be brought to battle. By 1937, the Russians had recreated the Mongol army in a doctrinal and tactical sense, and had designed and deployed new equipment—primarily the tank, combat support fighters, trucks (to transport infantry), and radios (to command units in prearranged battle drills)—to support this doctrine. The stimulus for this revolution in military thinking can be traced to Ivanin's analysis of methods of the Mongol armies. The institutionalization of the Mongol way of war in the Soviet army was due, more pragmatically, to two men, Marshall Tukhachevsky and Mikhail Vasilyevich Frunze (1885–1925).

Frunze was born in the Central Asian city of Bishkek, since renamed Frunze in his honor. Much of his early life was influenced by his knowledge and experience of the Mongol and Turkic peoples living around him who still practiced the methods of war associated with the steppe horse archers, both in their tribal conflicts and in their skirmishes with Russian authorities. He was a superior student who excelled at military history, and from an early time in his life, Frunze's favorite general was Tamerlane, the great Mongol khan who burned Moscow.[15] Frunze enrolled at the Academy at Vernyi, and graduated in 1904 with a gold medal for scholarship. A true military historian and intellectual, he joined the Bolsheviks during the civil war and distinguished himself as an excellent combat commander. In 1924, he was called to Moscow and made chairman of the Revolutionary Military Council, the commandant of the Staff College of the Red Army, where he had a profound influence on the curriculum, and Deputy People's Commissar for Military and Naval Affairs.

Frunze disagreed with Trotsky regarding the nature of the new Soviet army, and won the debate, creating a genuine Russian national army to defend the Soviet state. He was a great military theorist who laid down a new doctrinal basis for the Red Army of the mid-'20s. This new doctrine had been drawn directly from the Mongol experience of war, and we may rightly suspect the influence of Ivanin's work on Frunze's thinking, since it is hardly likely that such a well-known work of military history could have escaped his notice. Frunze's new doctrine had three themes: (1) the predominance of the offensive in war, (2) emphasis upon mobility and maneuver across great distances, and, as a logical corollary, (3) a major role for cavalry units in carrying out the doctrine. This last is easily explained by the fact that the tank had not yet reached a level of development where it could reasonably be expected to compete with the horse in terms of speed, maneuver, and, above all, range and reliability.

It fell to one of Frunze's colleagues to further refine the Mongol method of war in Soviet operational doctrine and to give it genuine institutional expression in the form of equipment design and application in war. The man who accomplished this was Mikhail Tukhachevsky, the Chief of Staff of the Red Army from 1925 until his death at the hands of Stalin's henchmen. Tukhachevsky had been born in Smolensk. He attended the Alexandrovsky Military Academy, where, we may reasonably assume, he read Ivanin's work as part of the standard military curriculum. He fought as a young officer in World War I and in the civil wars that followed. He rose rapidly in the ranks and became head of the Red Army Military Academy, where he wrote extensively on military history and strategy. In 1925, he was appointed Chief of Staff, where he formalized the new Soviet strategic and doctrinal concepts that had characterized his writings as a younger officer. Tukhachevsky was regarded during his lifetime as one of the great military thinkers of his day and as the most prominent military figure to have perished in Stalin's purges.[16]

Tukhachevsky professionalized the Soviet officer corps, removing scores of party hacks and ideologues from their posts, a development that probably led Stalin to distrust the senior officer corps considerably, and that led to their eventual destruction, almost to a man, in the purge of 1937. Tukhachevsky had followed the Mongol practice of awarding commands on the basis of experience and expertise, rather than on party or personal connections. He further developed some of Frunze's ideas, especially on mobility, speed, and maneuver, and anchored the Soviet army in the doctrine of the offensive as expressed in his own unique contribution of the Deep Battle. As chief of armaments, Tukhachevsky modernized the Soviet army, with great emphasis placed on the means to employ speed, mobility, and the offensive, all linked to immense firepower, that could maneuver across great distances and various types of terrain. Tukhachevsky began the great Soviet doctrinal emphasis on tanks to carry out the role played historically by Mongol cavalry. The cavalry formations that Frunze had stressed to carry out the same role were now obsolete, as the tank's reliability, speed, and firepower increased with each passing year. Tukhachevsky also placed great emphasis on the ability to deliver fire against enemy formations preparatory to the assault, the old Mongol idea of using light cavalry archers to soften up the tight formations of European and Chinese knights, before shattering them with the shock charge of the heavy cavalry. In the doctrine of Deep Battle, Soviet forward aviation provided the fire support for ground combat.

Although Tukhachevsky emphasized the role of artillery, as well, the lack of self-propelled guns and the lack of trucks to tow artillery pieces made its use somewhat problematic. Recognizing the role that infantry played in Mongol tactics, Tukhachevskii attempted to "motorize" Soviet infantry so that it could keep up with the rapidly moving tank columns. Unfortunately, Soviet industry was never able to meet the Red Army's requirements for trucks, and it was not until around 1943, when American Lend-Lease trucks began arriving in large numbers, that the Soviet infantry became significantly motorized. The armored personnel carrier had not yet been invented of course. Soviet military historians agree that of all the equipment provided to the Red Army by the West during World War II, the most important to the eventual victory were the trucks.[17]

By 1937, the Red Army was the largest and most mechanized army in Europe, and its commanders were better trained in the operational control of large units over great distances than any officer corps in the West. In a very real sense, Frunze and Tukhachevsky, both students of Ivanin's analysis of the Mongol campaigns, had reconfigured the Soviet army in the image of the army of Genghis Khan and Subotai. This was true strategically, tactically, and in the equipment employed to execute the doctrine of Deep Battle. Just as the Red Army was reaching its peak of combat power, disaster struck. Stalin turned his suspicions on the senior officer corps, executing thousands of officers and almost every one of the senior commanders, including Mikhail Tukhachevsky. With the senior commanders gone, the ability to command large units also went. The tank armies were broken up into smaller units, which were then dispersed to serve as support for the infantry, the same role played by cavalry in the traditional Russian army of World War I and in accordance with (then current) French practice. Talented commanders were replaced with political toadies without military expertise or experience.

In what surely ranks as one of the more bizarre developments in military history, the Soviet army reintroduced large horse cavalry formations, which suffered the same fate as the Polish cavalry when they attempted to stop a German armored attack with bravado and horseflesh. Within three years, the careful work of Frunze and Tukhachevsky to shape the Soviet army into a first-rate fighting force had been undone. And when war finally came, the Red Army collapsed.

During World War II, some of the old generals were released and put in command of the Soviet Army, which, by 1943, had begun to reacquire some of the tactical ability that it had lost. But it was after the war that the Red Army began to develop the concepts that underlay the doctrine of Deep Battle fully. Whereas, prior to the war, the Red Army had stressed the importance of the offensive and the Western armies the importance of the defense, during World War II the armies had switched doctrines. And after the war, they switched doctrines again.

The American and NATO forces in Europe had never really been a match for the Soviet Army, forcing them to develop a doctrine of defense in depth. To this end, American equipment design stressed its ability to destroy tanks moving in the offensive. Whereas Soviet helicopter design aimed at destroying American anti-tank guns and missile teams by attacking personnel, American helicopters were designed to kill tanks. Soviet forward aviation was configured to deliver forward area firepower in support of armored columns, while American aircraft stressed their role in destroying Soviet aircraft.

The Russian emphasis on the Mongol way of war could also be seen in their introduction of the armored personnel carrier and large numbers of self-propelled guns, both designed to provide infantry and fire support to the armored columns moving in the offensive. The same was true with the great emphasis the Soviets placed on communications, insisting upon equipping even the smallest units with radios. Like the Mongol army, Russian commanders and units were expected to execute a number of preplanned battle drills. The radio was the means of command and control of these drills, just as the flags and pennants had served the same function for Mongol field commanders. Even the Red Army's emphasis on the use of smoke to conceal battlefield maneuvers has its origins in the Mongol army's use of smoke for the same purposes. In a very real sense, the Mongol army was alive and well for most of the Cold War until its death in 1991, when the Soviet empire collapsed. There was little in the way of Soviet doctrine or in the manner in which Soviet commanders employed their modern equipment that would have surprised the wily old Subotai. He would have recognized it immediately for what it was, his own army reincarnated in the modern age.

When the Franciscan monk Giovanni di Plano Carpini visited the Mongol court in 1247, he reported that Subotai was still alive and in his early seventies. Carpini wrote that Subotai was, at that time, still regarded as the most famous and admired of all the Mongol generals.[18] The Mongols called him Subotai the Unfailing, and Carpini wrote that "he was a soldier without weakness."[19] Various sources offer only glimpses of the man's personality. The Muslims thought him "silent, insatiable, and remorseless," while the Russians said of him that he was "extremely disciplined."[20] By far, the most revealing description of Subotai is provided by the Chinese. They held Subotai in high esteem as a great warrior, and, upon his death, they bestowed upon him the title of King of Honan (Hunan Province), because he had captured this province in the war against the Chin. They also awarded him an honorific title calling him "faithful and steady."[21] And so it was that even his enemies respected his military ability. And rightly so; for his brilliance in planning and carrying out campaigns, Subotai the Valiant ranks among the greatest generals in military history.

Subotai died at age seventy-three. He had grown tired of the life at court. He had been sixty-eight when he returned from the long campaign against Hungary and the West, and now age was taking its toll. Subotai was disgusted by the political maneuvering of Batu and Kuyuk that went on after the death of Ogedai. He left the capital for an encampment on the banks of the Danube River.[22] Legend has it that he removed all his badges of rank from his yurt and spent his days tending his herds and watching his grandson, Achu, practice the skills of the Mongol warrior. The Danube is obviously far to the west of the Mongolian steppe, and it might seem strange that Subotai would have chosen to retire to so distant a place. It is possible that Subotai came to the banks of the Danube to be near his son, Uriangkatai, who served as one of Batu's officers. Batu's fiefdom was the Golden Horde, and included Russia and other lands along the Danube.[23] Sir Basil Liddell-Hart, quoting Muslim chroniclers, noted that at the time of his death, Subotai "had conquered thirty-two nations and won sixty-five pitched battles,"[24] a record of accomplishment literally unsurpassed by any of the great generals who had gone before him.

8 Postscript: The Lessons of Mongol Warfare

lthough I had long been interested in the Mongol armies, it was not until I assumed a professorship at the US Army War College that I could indulge my interest in more than a cursory manner. While at the college, I introduced the systematic study of ancient military history, a course that is still offered in the curriculum. When I taught the course, I hit upon the idea of having my students, all colonels or lieutenant colonels, study the ancient campaigns with a view toward extracting from their studies those strategic and tactical lessons that might be of use to the modern military commander. This was an effort to make history "live," insofar as my students might find the study of the past to be useful to their own military lives in the present. What follows is the list of strategic and tactical lessons that my students extracted from their studies of Subotai's campaigns. They seem, to me, just as valid today as they were some ten years ago, when they were originally compiled, and many of these lessons can be found incorporated into the classes used to instruct our next generation of field commanders at the US Army Command and General Staff College. Given the Mongol origins of these lessons, they may serve as a summary of Mongol military doctrine as derived from a study of the life, battle, tactics, and strategies of Subotai.

STRATEGY

- The application of military force, if sufficiently sudden and violent, often paralyzes political will. Accordingly, a rival military coalition can be prevented from forming if one strikes in such a manner as to demonstrate to potential rival coalition members that the risks of resistance are too great. The Mongols employed this principle in their invasion of Russia. The rapid and complete destruction of the northern Russian states paralyzed the ability of the southern Russian states to resist the next step of the invasion.

■ Devise and utilize a strategic vision, for it is strategic vision that shapes goals, ways, and means. The Mongols' military campaigns each made sense in terms of their specific relationship to their larger strategic vision, a strategic vision that remained unchanged, in its essentials, for almost a century.

■ Strategic intelligence is perhaps the most valuable asset at a commander's disposal in planning the operational conduct of a campaign. In the case of the Mongols, the strategic intelligence assessment guided the entire planning process. Strategic intelligence provides the basis for strategic vision and for developing the military component of the overall strategy. The collection of strategic intelligence is especially important during times of prolonged peace.

■ The institutionalization of military excellence is a valuable element of national power. A study of the Mongol campaigns reveals that a well-led and well-trained army, although smaller, will almost always defeat a larger army that is poorly led. The pursuit of excellence in the leadership ranks of the military establishment is an important goal for the society-at-large. An army of donkeys led by a lion is more effective than an army of lions led by a donkey!

■ The primacy of politics in military affairs is absolute, and often works against military effectiveness. Although the armies of the European states greatly outnumbered the Mongol invaders, these states were unable to reconcile their political and religious differences to come to the aid of Hungary. In planning military operations, the effect of political realities upon the enemy's ability to fight can be crucial.

■ Resist the temptation to permit operational success to skew strategy from its original goal(s). After the battle of Liegnitz, all of Europe lay open to Mongol invasion. Yet, the Mongol commander, Kaidu Khan, did not pursue the defeated enemy. Kaidu remained concentrated upon the strategic plan, and moved his troops to Hungary to support the invasion, as planned. For the same reason, Subotai did not attack Novgorod when he had the chance, but stuck to the larger strategic objective. Battlefield success always presents the risk of forcing a change in strategic objectives.

■ Battles do not occur in isolation from the rest of the enemy population, civilian or military. At the beginning of a campaign, it is important that you determine what psychological message you wish to convey to the general enemy population. In the case of the Mongols, they sought to strike terror in the general populace. In other circumstances, the struggle for the "hearts and minds" of the population may be more appropriate. In either case, the question must be addressed: How should one's military operations influence the thought processes and values of the enemy population?

■ Avoid the trap of protecting useless and/or helpless allies. Protecting allies who cannot make a significant contribution to their own defense or the common combat effort only ensures that you will inherit all their enemies and few of their friends. The Russians and King Bela both provided protection for the Cumans with the major result of bringing down the wrath of the Mongols. Allies are not friends in the same sense that individuals are friends. Successful alliances are premised on mutual interests and resources.

■ While diplomacy always guides military strategy, there are times when diplomacy can be used correctly as a tool of military strategy as well. Diplomacy can be very helpful in fragmenting a hostile military coalition. The Mongols used diplomacy brilliantly in this regard when they shattered the coalition of tribal armies that opposed their passage over the Caucasus Mountains. Divide and conquer! Use diplomacy to drive wedges into the political structure of a rival alliance or military coalition.

■ Make full use of a plan for strategic deception. The proper thought planted in the mind of the enemy can be worth several divisions. The Mongols always used a plan of strategic deception that was carefully tailored to their operational goals, usually with great success.

TACTICS

■ Never go into the attack without first concentrating and coordinating your forces at the objective. Mstislav the Daring forgot this at the Kalka River and committed his forces piecemeal, allowing a numerically inferior enemy force to defeat his much larger army.

■ Be aware of and use the effects of weather to enhance combat power. European armies during the Middle Ages did not usually fight during the winter months. This limitation permitted the Mongols to increase their military power by taking the field in winter, where the frozen terrain neutralized the defensive value of streams, rivers, and swamps.

■ Never allow the desire to seize the initiative and move boldly into the attack to cloud your analysis of the situation in which you must fight. King George IV of Georgia and Henry the Pious both went into the attack before adequately assessing the nature and deployment of the forces they faced, with the result that both had their armies destroyed. Do not die from enthusiasm!

■ Appreciate the importance of the ambush; it is often the cheapest and most effective way to destroy an enemy force. Mongol commanders developed the ambush into high art. The ambush is normally thought of as the domain of the guerrilla, but the ambush is a particularly valuable form of combat for a highly mobile army that can concentrate quickly at the objective.

■ Find ways to obscure the battlefield to cover your deployment and maneuver. At both the battle of Liegnitz and the Kalka River, the Mongols used smoke to cover their counterattacks. In both instances, the enemy was caught unprepared. Maximize concealment on the battlefield.

■ Even after a success on the battlefield, give proper attention to sustaining your lines of communication. After the great victory at Kiev, but prior to the invasion of Hungary, Subotai detailed a large segment of his army to guard his lines of communication.

■ Conduct a pursuit with audacity and lethality. Once you have the enemy on the run, move quickly to destroy him or break his will to resist.

■ Emulate Subotai! When the joining of two forces will put you at a disadvantage, move decisively to engage and destroy one of them. If done successfully, the defeat of one force is usually sufficient to make it unnecessary to engage the second force. Do not allow a superior force to concentrate in your area of operations if you can prevent it by aggressive action.

■ Sometimes it is better to leave a surrounded enemy an avenue of retreat rather than cut him off entirely. As long as there is a way to survive, it is always possible that the enemy can be made to surrender. The psychology of survival is an important element in human motivation; use it to your advantage.

■ Follow the Mongol practical maxim of "march divided, fight united" by developing the ability to rapidly concentrate your forces opposite the enemy before the enemy can react.

- An army is the instrument of the will of a single commander. The purpose of maintaining communication among various elements of an army is to permit the commander's will to direct the operational conduct of the army. Follow the example of Subotai (again).

- Never let communications paralyze command. The ability of an army to communicate should never be allowed to degenerate into micromanagement by the army commander, or his staff, of lower-level combat operations. Once a unit commander has been given his objectives, allow him to choose his own means to achieve those objectives. Follow the example of the Mongol commanders and the German General staff—employ mission orders and practice *Auftragstaktik*.

- Remember the failure of King Bela at the Sajo River. Always provide for sufficient tactical depth in your defensive position.

- Never lose contact with an enemy force or segment of that force that is deployed against you. Bela lost contact with three *toumans* of Batu's army at the Sajo River, and they struck him in the flank and destroyed his army. Know where the enemy is at all times.

- Befriend your staff artillery officer. Nothing kills or confuses like artillery! The Mongols made extensive and innovation use of artillery as an integral part of their battle plans.

- Imitate Subotai. Always go where they least expect you to go.

NOTES

CHAPTER 1: SUBOTAI THE VALIANT

1. There are two English translations of *The Secret History of the Mongols*. The more detailed and academic treatment of the famous Mongol epic is by Francis Woodman Cleaves, published by Harvard University Press in 1982. The other is by Paul Kahn, published by Northpoint Press, San Francisco, in 1984, and is a more poetic translation. There are, as far as I am able to discern, no serious contradictions between the two works. All quotes from the epic that appear in this work are from Kahn's translation, unless otherwise noted. Paul Kahn, *The Secret History of the Mongols* (San Francisco: Northpoint Press, 1984), 134.

2. *Secret History*, 32 and 134.

3. Ibid.

4. Ibid.

5. *Secret History*, 125.

6. Rene Grousset, *The Empire of the Steppes* (New Brunswick, NJ: Rutgers University Press, 1970), 582.

7. Ibid., 579.

8. Harold Lamb, *The March of the Barbarians* (New York: Literary Guild of America, 1940), 376. This source must be used with caution, since it is, in essence, more a historical novel than a genuine history. However, Lamb's academic abilities as both an historian and linguist of Muslim and Chinese sources cannot be denied. The footnotes and the excursus which appear at the back of the book can be relied upon as well as any other competent historian of the period can be relied upon.

9. Ibid.

10. Friar Giovanni Di Plano Carpini, *The Story of the Mongols Whom We Call Tartars* [translated by Erik Hildinger] (Boston: Branden Publishing Company, 1996), 65.

11. Jean Pierre Abel Remusat, *Nouveaux Melanges Asiatiques: Etudes Biographiques,* vol. 2 (Schubart et Heideloff, Paris, 1829), 97.

12. Once more, the reader is reminded of the two translations of the *Secret History.*

13. *Secret History*, 47.

14. Ibid., 50–51.

15. The first documented case of the use of the commander's conference by an army in antiquity is by Thutmose III, before his attack on Megiddo.

16. *Secret History*, 50.

17. Remusat, 90.

18. From "*If*," by Rudyard Kipling.

19. For the role of intellect in military leadership, see Richard A. Gabriel, *Great Captains of Antiquity* (Westport, CT: Greenwood Press, 2001), Chapter 8 "On The Origins of Great Captains."

20. R. P. Lister, *Genghis Khan* (New York: Dorset Press, 1969), 137. Charlemagne, too, disposed of an excess of Saxons in the same manner.

21. Rene Grousset, *Conqueror of the World: The Life of Genghis Khan* (New York: Orion Press, 1966), 135.

22. Ibid., 134; see also Cleaves, 39.

23. Ibid.

24. *Secret History*, 106.

25. Ibid., 107.

26. Ibid., 108–109.

27. Ibid., 110.

28. Napoleon often advanced with his units in thick columns for exactly the same reasons.

29. Grousset, *Conqueror of the World*, 152.

30. *Secret History*, 111.

31. Ibid.

32. Ibid., 114.

33. Ibid., 115.

34. Ibid., 118.

35. Ibid., 118; Grousset, *Conqueror of the World*, 161.

36. Richard A. Gabriel, *The Great Armies of Antiquity* (Westport, CT: Greenwood Press, 2002), 108, 118. For more detail on David's chariots, see also (by the same author), *The Military History of Ancient Israel* (Westport, CT: Greenwood Press, 2003), Chapter 2.

37. Lister, 180.

38. *Secret History*, 118.

39. Ibid.

40. Ibid., 119.

41. Ibid.

42. Ibid.

43. Ibid.

44. Ibid., 147.

45. Ibid., 125.

46. George Vernadsky, *The Mongols and Russia* (New Haven: Yale University Press, 1953), 29.

47. Grousset, *Conqueror of the World*, 169.

48. *Secret History*, 140.

CHAPTER 2: THE MONGOL WAR MACHINE

1. R. P. Lister, *Genghis Khan* (New York: Dorset Press, 1965), 185. See also David Morgan, *The Mongols* (Oxford, UK: Blackwell, 1986), 55–61.

2. Paul Kahn, *The Secret History of the Mongols: An Adaptation* (San Francisco: Northpoint Press, 1984), 140. The more definitive and academic work on the subject is by Francis Woodman Cleaves, *The Secret History of the Mongols* (Cambridge, MA: Harvard University Press, 1982). I have used both sources extensively in this book.

3. Richard A. Gabriel and Donald W. Boose Jr., *Great Battles of Antiquity* (Westport, CT: Greenwood Press, 1994), 536.

4. Morgan, Chapter 4; also, S. R. Turnbull and Angus McBride, *The Mongols* (London: Osprey Publishers, 1988), 22.

5. Morgan, 87.

6. Harold Lamb, *Genghis Khan* (New York: Doubleday, 1927), Chapters 1 and 2 provide a good description of the how difficult the life of the Mongols was (especially for Mongol children.

7. Ibid., 201–204 for a list of the laws of the *Yassak*.

8. *Secret History*, 140.

9. For more on the armor, weapons, and equipment of the Mongol soldier, see Michael Edwards and James L. Stanfield, "Lord of the Mongols: Genghis Khan," *National Geographic*, vol. 190, no. 6 (December, 1996), 14–16; Turnbull and McBride, 13–22; and Gabriel and Boose, 539–541.

10. Edwards and Stanfield, 13.

11. Gabriel and Boose, 541; also James Chambers, *The Devil's Horsemen: The Mongol Invasion of Europe* (New York: Atheneum, 1979), 56.

12. Turnbull and McBride, 17.

13. Morgan, 84.

14. Chambers, 59.

15. Edwards and Stanfield, 32–33.

16. Chambers, 55.

17. Turnbull and McBride, 30.

18. Chambers, 62. See also Edwards and Stanfield, 32, for a good graphic portrayal of the Mongol camp and the army on the move.

19. Gabriel and Boose, 545–547.

20. Giovanni di Plano Carpini, *The Story of the Mongols Whom We Call The Tartars* (translated by Erik Hildinger; Boston: Brandon Publishing Company, 1996), Chapter 6. B. H. Liddell Hart, *Great Captains Unveiled* (London: Blackwood and Sons, 1927), 28.

21. Gabriel and Boose, 545–547.

22. Chambers, 60–61.

CHAPTER 3: THE WARS AGAINST THE CHIN

1. Michael Prawdin, *The Mongol Empire* (London: George Allen Ltd., 1940), 102.

2. E. D. Phillips, *The Mongols* (New York: Frederick A. Praeger, 1969), 56.

3. Rene Grousset, *The Empire of the Steppes* (New Brunswick, NJ: Rutgers University Press, 1970), 228.

4. Ibid.

5. Prawdin, 102.

6. Ibid., 109.

7. Unfortunately, we have no information regarding the size of a Chin "division," but we may well assume that it was probably several thousand men.

8. Prawdin, 129.

9. W. E. Henthorn, *Korea: The Mongol Invasions* (Leiden: E. J. Brill, 1963), ix–x.

10. Ibid.

11. Jean Pierre Abel Remusat, *Nouveaux Melanges Asiatiques: Etudes Biographiques*, vol. 2 (Paris: Schubart et Heideloff, 1829), 93. Remusat's account is based on the Chinese text entitled *Sou-Houng-Kian-Lou,* which Remusat translated.

12. Harold Lamb, *The March of the Barbarians* (New York: Doubleday, 1940), 104.

13. Remusat, 93.

14. Lamb, 113.

15. Remusat, 95.

CHAPTER 4: HURRICANE FROM THE EAST

1. Leo De Hartog, *Genghis Khan: Conqueror of the World* (New York: Barnes and Noble, 1999), 89. See also Rene Grousset, *The Empire of the Mongols* (Paris, 1941), 197, and J. A. Boyle, "Dynastic and Political History of the Il-Khans," in *Cambridge History of Iran*, vol. 5, *The Saljuq and Mongol Periods* (Cambridge, England: 1968), p. 305.

2. Hartog, 89.

3. Ibid., 90; see also A. Hartman, "An Nasir il-Din Allah (1180–1225): *Politik, Religion, Kultur in der Spaeten Abbasidenzeit*" (Berlin: 1975), 84.

4. Trevor N. Dupuy, *The Military Life of Genghis Khan* (New York: Franklin Watts, Inc., 1969), 66.

5. Michael Prawdin, *The Mongol Empire* (London: George Allen and Unwin Ltd., 1940), 159.

6. J. J. Saunders, *The History of the Mongol Conquests* (Philadelphia, PA: University of Pennsylvania Press, 1971), 55–56.

7. Ibid., 54.

8. Prawdin, 156.

9. Hartog, 98.

10. Harold Lamb, *The March of the Barbarians* (New York: Literary Guild of America, 1940), 60.

11. Prawdin, 160.

12. Lamb, 124.

13. J. A. Boyle, *The History of the World Conqueror by Ala-ad-din Malik Juvaini* (Manchester, England: 1958), 100–102.

14. Prawdin, 171–172.

15. Ibid., 188.

16. Rene Grousset, *The Empire Of The Steppes: A History of Central Asia* (New Brunswick, New Jersey: Rutgers University Press, 1970), 241.

17. Ibid. Grousset cites the original sources from Juvaini and Rashid ad-Din in support here.

18. Ibid. Again, Grousset cites the original sources.

CHAPTER 5: THE GREAT CAVALRY RAID

1. Rene Grousset, *Conqueror of the World: The Life of Genghis Khan* (New York: Orion Books, 1966), 265.

2. Harold Lamb, *Genghis Khan* (New York: Doubleday, 1927), 114.

3. James Chambers, *The Devil's Horsemen: The Mongol Invasion of Europe* (New York: Atheneum, 1979), 20.

4. Richard A. Gabriel and Donald W. Boose, Jr., *Great Battles of Antiquity: A Strategic and Tactical Guide to the Great Battles that Shaped the Development of War* (Westport, CT: Greenwood Press, 1994), 524.

5. Chambers, 20.

6. J. J. Saunders, *The History of the Mongol Conquests* (Philadelphia: University of Pennsylvania Press, 1971), 59.

7. Gabriel and Boose, 525.

8. Michael Prawdin, *The Mongol Empire* (London: Allen and Unwin, Ltd., 1940), 212.

9. Grousset, 266.

10. Ibid.

11. Chambers, 24.

12. Ibid.

13. Prawdin, 217.

14. Leo De Hartog, *Genghis Khan: Conqueror of the World* (New York: Barnes and Noble, 1989), 122.

15. W. Barthold, *Four Studies on the History of Central Asia*, vol. 1 (Leiden: Brill, 1956), 41.

CHAPTER 6: THE ATTACK ON THE WEST

1. Richard A. Gabriel and Donald W. Boose, Jr., *The Great Battles of Antiquity: A Strategic and Tactical Guide to the Great Battles that Shaped the Development of War* (Westport, CT: Greenwood Press, 1994), 530.

2. George Vernadsky, *Kievan Russia* (New Haven, CT: Yale University Press, 1948), 193.

3. Ibid., 194.

4. James Chambers, *The Devil's Horsemen* (New York: Atheneum, 1979), 71.

5. J. J. Saunders, *The History of the Mongol Conquests* (Philadelphia, PA: University of Pennsylvania Press, 1971), 82.

6. Ibid., 80; also see footnote 30 of that chapter in Saunders for more on the source of the quotation.

7. Ibid.

8. Harold Lamb, *The March of the Barbarians* (New York: Literary Guild of America, 1940), 136.

9. Chambers, 75.

10. Lamb, 137.

11. Saunders, 83.

12. Gabriel and Boose, 531.

13. Chambers, 81.

14. Gabriel and Boose, 533.

15. Erik Hildinger, "The Mongol Invasion of Europe," 39 *Military History* (June, 1997), 41.

16. Ibid., 42.

17. Gabriel and Boose, 549.

18. Vernadsky, 192.

19. Ibid.

20. Lamb, 134.

21. Gabriel and Boose, 553.

22. Ibid., 556.

CHAPTER 7: THE MONGOL MILITARY LEGACY

1. Harold Lamb, *The March of the Barbarians* (New York: Literary Guild of America, 1940), 344.

2. George Vernadsky, *The Mongols and Russia* (New Haven: Yale University Press, 1953), 119.

3. Giovanni di Plano Carpini, *The Story of the Mongols Whom We Call the Tartars* (Boston: Branden Publishing, 1996).

4. Hans Delbruck, *The History of the Art of War*, trans. by Walter J. Renfroe, Jr. 4 vols. (Westport, CT: Greenwood Press, 1980).

5. Vernadsky, 119.

6. Ibid.

7. B. H. Liddell-Hart, *Great Captains Unveiled* (London: William Blackwood and Sons, 1927), 33.

8. Vernadsky, 120.

9. Frederick Kagan, "Soviet Operational Art: The Theory and Practice of Initiative, 1917–1945," in Christopher Kolenda, *Leadership: The Warrior's Art* (Carlisle, PA: Army War College Foundation Press, 2001), 227.

10. Ibid.

11. Liddell-Hart, 32.

12. Kagan, 228.

13. Ibid., 230.

14. Kagan, 230.

15. Joseph L. Wieczynski (ed.), *The Modern Encyclopedia of Russian and Soviet History*, vol. 40 (Gulf Breeze, FL: Academic International Press, 1985), 38.

16. *The Modern Encyclopedia of Russian and Soviet History*, vol. 12 (1979) 81.

17. I am indebted to the distinguished historian of Russia, John Windhausen, for informing me of the importance of the Lend-Lease trucks in the view of Soviet historians.

18. Carpini, 65.

19. The translation of Carpini's words is from Lamb, 191.

20. Ibid., 30.

21. Remusat, 97.

22. Ibid.

23. In 1257, Uriangkatai led an army against the kingdom of Annam (Vietnam), with its capital at Hanoi, which he plundered in December of that year. McNeil has argued that the Great Plague, which struck Europe shortly thereafter, had its origins in Southeast Asia, from whence it had been brought back to Central Asia by Mongol armies and transmitted from there by Genoese ships trading at Odessa (on the Black Sea). It may well have been Uriangkatai's army that brought the plague with it upon its return to Central Asia.

24. Basil H. Liddell-Hart, *Great Captains Unveiled* (London: William Blackwood and Sons, 1927), 30.

FURTHER READING

Barthold, W. *Four Studies on the History of Central Asia*, vol. 1. Leiden: E. J. Brill, 1956.

Boyle, J. A. "Dynastic and Political History of the Il-Khans," in *Cambridge History of Iran*, vol. 5, *The Saljuq and Mongol Periods*. Cambridge, 1968, pp. 300–317.

Boyle, J. A. *The History of the World Conqueror by Ala-ad-din Malik Juvaini*. Manchester, England, 1958. *Cambridge Medieval History*, vol. 4 (1966) and vol. 6 (1968).

Chambers, James. *The Devil's Horsemen*. New York: Atheneum, 1979.

Cleaves, F. W. *The Secret History of the Mongols*. (trans.) Cambridge, MA: Blackwell, 1982.

De Hartog, Leo. *Genghis Khan: Conqueror of the World*. New York: Barnes and Noble, 1999.

Dupuy, R. Ernest and Trevor N. *Encyclopedia of Military History*. New York: Harper and Rowe, 1986.

Dupuy, Trevor N. *The Military Life of Genghis Khan*. New York: Franklin Watts, Inc., 1969.

Edwards, Michael and James L. Stanfield. "Lord of the Mongols: Genghis Khan," *National Geographic*, vol. 190 (December, 1996), pp. 14–23.

Gabriel, Richard A. and Donald W. Boose, Jr. *The Great Battles of Antiquity: A Strategic and Tactical Guide to the Great Battles that Shaped the Development of War*. Westport, CT: Greenwood Press, 1994.

Grousset, Rene. *The Empire of the Mongols*. Paris, 1941.

Grousset, Rene. *Conqueror of the World: The Life of Genghis Khan*. New York: Orion Press, 1966.

Grousset, Rene. *The Empire of the Steppes*. New Brunswick, NJ: Rutgers University Press, 1970.

Hartman, A. "An Nasir il-Din Allah (1180–1225): *Politik, Religion, Kultur in der Spaeten Abbasidenzeit.*" Berlin, 1975.

Henthorn, W. E. *Korea: The Mongol Invasions*. Leiden: E. J. Brill, 1963.

Hildinger, Erik. "The Mongol Invasion of Europe," *Military History*, 39 (June, 1997), pp. 40–46.

Kagan, Frederick, "Soviet Operational Art: The Theory and Practice of Initiative, 1917–1945," in Christopher Kolenda, *Leadership: The Warrior's Art*. Carlisle, PA: Army War College Foundation Press, 2001, pp. 225–248.

Kahn, Paul. *The Secret History of the Mongols*. San Francisco: Northpoint Press, 1984.

Kiss, Peter A. "Horsemen of Cruel Cunning," *Military History* (December, 1986), pp. 34–41.

Laffont, Robert. *The Ancient Art of War*, vol. 2. New York: Time-Life, 1966.

Lamb, Harold. *Genghis Khan*. New York: Doubleday, 1927.

Lamb, Harold. *The March of the Barbarians*. New York: Literary Guild of America, 1940.

Liddell-Hart, Sir Basil H. *Great Captains Unveiled*. London: William Blackwood and Sons, 1927.

Lister, R. P. *Genghis Khan*. New York: Dorset Press, 1969.

Martin, H. D. "The Mongol Army," *Journal of the Royal Asiatic Society*, vol. 1 (1943), pp. 46–85.

Morgan, David. *The Mongols*. Cambridge, MA: Blackwell, 1986.

Oman, Sir Charles. *The Art of War in the Middle Ages*, vol. 2. London: Greenhill, 1924.

Plano Carpini, Giovanni di. *The Story of the Mongols Whom We Call the Tartars*. [translated by Erik Hildinger] Boston: Branden Publishing Company, 1996.

Prawdin, Michael. *The Mongol Empire*. London: George Allen and Unwin Ltd., 1940.

Phillips, E. D. *The Mongols*. New York: Frederick Praeger, 1969.

Remusat, Jean Pierre Abel. *Nouveaux Melanges Asiatiques: Etudes Biographiques*, vol. 2. Paris: Schubart et Heideloff, 1829, pp. 89–97.

Saunders, J. J. *The History of the Mongol Conquests*. Philadelphia: University of Pennsylvania Press, 1971.

Sinor, D. "The Inner Asian Warriors," *Journal of the American Oriental Society,* 101/102 (1981), pp. 133–144.

Turnbull, S. R. *The Mongols*. London: Osprey, 1980.

Vernadsky, George. *Kievan Russia*. New Haven, CT: Yale University Press, 1948.

Vernadsky, George. *The Mongols and Russia*. New Haven, CT: Yale University Press, 1953.

Vickers, Ralph. "The Mongols and Their Impact on the Medieval West," *Strategy and Tactics* (March/April, 1979), pp. 23–28.

Wieczynski, Joseph L. (ed.) *The Modern Encyclopedia of Russian and Soviet History,* vols. 12 and 40. Gulf Breeze, FL: Academic International Press, 1958.

INDEX

ABOUT THE AUTHOR

RICHARD A. GABRIEL is a historian and Adjunct Professor of Humanities and Ethics at Daniel Webster College. He is the author of thirty-five books, including *The Great Battles of Antiquity, The Great Armies of Antiquity,* and *The Great Captains of Antiquity.* His most recent work is *The Military History of Ancient Israel.* He was a professor at St. Anslem College for more than twenty years before assuming the position of Professor of History and Politics at the U.S. Army War College where he introduced the first courses in ancient military history into the college curriculum.

OTHER BOOKS
BY RICHARD A. GABRIEL

The Military History of Ancient Israel
Great Armies of Antiquity
Sebastian's Cross
Gods of Our Fathers: The Memory of Egypt in Judaism and Christianity
Warrior Pharaoh
Great Captains of Antiquity
Great Battles of Antiquity
A Short History of War: Evolution of Warfare and Weapons
History of Military Medicine: Ancient Times to the Middle Ages
History of Military Medicine: Renaissance to the Present
From Sumer to Rome: The Military Capabilities of Ancient Armies
The Culture of War: Invention and Early Development
The Painful Field: Psychiatric Dimensions of Modern War
No More Heroes: Madness and Psychiatry in War
The Last Centurion
Military Psychiatry: A Comparative Perspective
Soviet Military Psychiatry
Military Incompetence: Why the US Military Doesn't Win
Operation Peace for Galilee: The Israeli-PLO War in Lebanon
The Antagonists: An Assessment of the Soviet and American Soldier
The Mind of the Soviet Fighting Man
Fighting Armies: NATO and the Warsaw Pact
Fighting Armies: Antagonists of the Middle East
Fighting Armies: Armies of the Third World
To Serve with Honor: A Treatise on Military Ethics
The New Red Legions: An Attitudinal Portrait of the Soviet Soldier
The New Red Legions: A Survey Data Sourcebook
Managers and Gladiators: Directions of Change in the Army
Crisis in Command: Mismanagement in the Army
Ethnic Groups in America
Program Evaluation: A Social Science Approach
The Ethnic Factor in the Urban Polity
The Environment: Critical Factors in Strategy Development